THE
BLACK BELT
LIBRARIAN

ALA Editions purchases fund advocacy, awareness, and accreditation programs for library professionals worldwide.

THE
BLACK BELT
LIBRARIAN

REAL-WORLD SAFETY & SECURITY

WARREN GRAHAM

American Library Association | Chicago   2012

WARREN GRAHAM has worked as a security professional for more than twenty-five years, seventeen as the security manager of the Public Library of Charlotte and Mecklenburg County, North Carolina. Graham left the library in 2006 to establish Warren Davis Graham Training and Consulting. He has made countless presentations and is a leading speaker internationally on practical day-to-day library security procedures. Contact Graham for training and consulting through his website: www.blackbeltlibrarians.com.

Printed in the United States of America
16 15 14 13 12   5 4 3 2 1

Extensive effort has gone into ensuring the reliability of the information in this book; however, the publisher makes no warranty, express or implied, with respect to the material contained herein.

ISBNs: 978-0-8389-1137-2 (paper); 978-0-8389-9373-6 (PDF); 978-0-8389-9374-3 (ePub); 978-0-8389-9375-0 (Mobipocket); 978-0-8389-9376-7 (Kindle). For more information on digital formats, visit the ALA Store at alastore.ala.org and select eEditions.

LIBRARY OF CONGRESS CATALOGING-IN-PUBLICATION DATA
Library of Congress Cataloging-in-Publication Data available at http://catalog.loc.gov/.

Book design in Fanwood and Novecento by Casey Bayer
Cover illustration © Csaba Peterdi/Shutterstock, Inc.

∞ This paper meets the requirements of ANSI/NISO Z39.48-1992 (Permanence of Paper).

For my coworkers on Planet Library, especially the librarian who once left me this anonymous note before one of my presentations:

*"Where in the library is the most appropriate place
for crazy people to hang out?"*

CONTENTS

The opinions expressed in this book are my own and do not necessarily reflect those of any previous or current employer of mine. But they should.

PREFACE

MUCH HAS CHANGED in the library world since I started consulting full time five years ago. Most libraries are facing serious budget cuts. Staffs are being reduced, and hours of operation are being lessened. At the same, libraries are busier than ever. With the nation's unemployment rate high, library resources are in serious demand.

With increased usage usually comes an increase in behavior problems. You can sit back and list the reasons for erratic behavior and give patrons all the excuses you want, but the bottom line is that the library environment still must be maintained. And to the average Joe, that means an atmosphere conducive to reading, research, studying, and learning.

I was quite excited to be asked by ALA to help provide them with updated editions of my two books. It is a great honor for me, a nonlibrarian, to be asked to do so. It has given me the opportunity to go back through the text to tweak and expand many points. It also assists me in what I set out to do originally by forming my own consulting company: to help as many librarians and library staff as I could by providing them with information that I know from my own experiences would immediately improve their workplace. The book is intended as a quick read to aid you daily as a reference and training guide.

There is often a huge gap between a library concept and the concept's application in a realistic, functioning way. This information will help you bridge that gap. I have never said that my way is the only way, but it is indeed a proven way. In the

Public Library of Charlotte and Mecklenburg County, working with the director who hired me to solve the mystery of behavior problems in the library, Robert Cannon, we proved it could be done—even in an environment that was most dire in the beginning. What has been quite interesting to me is that, in all my journeys all over North America, I have not seen one reason to change the way we approached security. If I started working at your library today, I would follow these same procedures.

No library wants problem patrons, but they are coming. I for one would rather be ready for them.

ACKNOWLEDGMENTS

THANKS TO MY grandmother, Mary Flowers, whom I often quote in my seminar. She was always there for me with constant love whenever I needed her. I miss her every day. She saved the child.

Thanks to my high school guidance counselor, William "Bill" Lindsay, who took time to listen to a lost and petrified high school senior. He encouraged my college education and was the first adult to tell me I had potential. He saved the teenager.

And thanks to my wife Jessica, who is even more beautiful on the *inside*. I would not be writing this were it not for her encouragement. I couldn't accomplish much without her. She saved the man.

INTRODUCTION

CHARLOTTE AND MECKLENBURG County library director Robert Cannon called me up one afternoon during my duties as security manager for an uptown mall that was situated right across the street from the main library. The library was closed temporarily, being refurbished and expanded from 60,000 to 160,000 square feet. He asked me how I went about controlling the many potential problems in my facility. He then quickly stole me away. Two weeks later, I was working for the library, only one short month before its grand reopening.

The late Nina Lyon, the finest overall librarian I have ever known and then manager of the main library building, took me on a tour and laid out the situation. She told me that in the old building she had to handle multiple security situations every single day. There had been no formal rules for library use and no consistency in the attempts to control behavior. The library had gone through several contract security companies that had all categorically failed. There was no standardized record keeping, and most of the daily "patrons" were using the building not as a library but as a home.

"But, what could really happen in here?" I silently asked myself as I was given a tour of the main library. Could they really be having the level of problems that was being described to me? Or was I simply working with a bunch of frightened librarians who were afraid of their own shadows?

To my genuine surprise, it was soon evident that the former was indeed the case. On the library's grand reopening day, after the building had been closed for two years of renovation, I can honestly say I was astounded at the situations I encountered. Intermingled with the majority of patrons, who were there for all the right reasons and enjoying the facility, were a mix of behavior problems than ran the gamut from the innocuous to the insane.

There were people who apparently had waited patiently for the previous twenty-four months to take a bath in our restrooms. Someone actually asked me if he could rent a shower. Many children ran rampant like baby cheetahs, and it was their oblivious parents who were at fault. More than a few thought this was a new library in every sense, and thus they owed nothing for lost or overdue materials. A few perverts experimented with new techniques of staring through the stacks at female patrons. One fine fellow actually had a small mirror duct-taped to the top of his shoe to facilitate looking up skirts, but only of patrons who were at least fifty years of age! And to round it all off, there was a good dose of genuinely disturbed people who had nowhere else to go and nothing else to do but come visit us. One fellow had a briefcase full of metal washers. He just wanted to sit at a table and see how high he could stack them, and he told everyone in no uncertain terms to stay away from him.

Though a few of the staff thought we should never ban or deny access to anyone no matter what they did, I countered by saying that they *would* be denying access to the regular, true library user if they didn't control the environment and keep it conducive to library use. Yes, it is indeed a public building, but what type? Well, it's a bloody *library*, and it should look and feel like one. It's not a place for people to come in and do anything they want. Just because we are a "public building" doesn't mean you can build a campfire in the middle of nonfiction.

We were successful in our security efforts thanks to my development of a solid, *simple* program and procedures. We involved all of the employees and trained them properly. We were more than fair in our advising patrons of the rules, and most important, from day one, we made sure that we treated *everyone* the same.

A few years later, a librarian called the director with a problem. A speaker on security had canceled at the last minute on a talk he was to give at the PLA conference in Atlanta, and the caller wanted to know if Bob was aware of anyone who could fill in. In a very short three days, I was standing in front of a couple thousand librarians, literally crammed into a ballroom, presenting my first talk on the subject of day-to-day safety in the library.

That's how my second career started, and since that day I have traveled the nation, training thousands of library staff. I always thought my home state of North Carolina had some rural areas, but I have visited some *extremely* remote library locations.

In one presentation out west, I was describing how one should go about calling 911 to solicit the best response. This petite, elderly attendee gently raised her hand and sweetly but anxiously asked, "But son, what if you don't have 911?" That was news to this city fellow. I had always thought having access to a 911 emergency response was a given.

Another time I was being driven from library to library by a director who had to stop the car and honk to get the buzzards out of the middle of the road. I had never seen a buzzard and had to ask what they were. I mean, it's not like we were in the desert, and I thought that was the only place buzzards lived.

In another state, we stopped at a convenience store filled with customers, and each and every one of them stopped pumping gas, playing video games, buying beer, or whatever else they were doing and just stared at me. The cashier actually had her mouth open. "Not from around here, are you, boy?" a gentleman dressed in overalls but no shirt asked me, as he completed his Slim Jim and Mountain Dew purchase. The dinner of champions.

And I will never forget the first time I traveled to a state far up north (which will remain unnamed here). The South has always had the reputation for having all the good ol' boys, but I will tell you that I saw more Confederate car license plates and stickers on this visit than I had ever seen before at home. Quite the eye-opener.

You name it. Go ahead, name it. I have more than likely either heard or personally witnessed it—on my own or in someone else's library. On the very serious end of things, I responded to a police call at one of our branches early one morning just a couple of months before I retired. The landscaping crew for a neighboring building discovered a body lying on the steps of an outside storytime area, located just by our children's area. Tragically, a twenty-one-year-old had committed suicide by shooting himself. Worse than the terrible effects of the bullet was the sight of such a young person who had given up before his life really began. I will never forget how much that affected me.

On the opposite end of the spectrum, during the late afternoon of the very same day, back at the main library, I was called to the computer area. A woman had screamed "Fire!" several times and was acting erratically. It turned out that she felt she was not receiving the level of help with her computer that she expected and had yelled to get some attention. Of course, the attention she received from me was not quite what she had in mind.

I think that was the day I decided to leave and did so soon after, in August 2006. After twenty-five years in security work, I was simply weary of it all and realized that I had been for several years. I was ready to help others learn how to handle these situations, and the demand for me to come and train staff was higher than ever.

You may be surprised to hear me say that I do not consider myself a security "expert," even though a lot of folks refer to me that way. Actually, I don't believe there is any such thing, and I will explain.

First, there is no way you can keep up with the physical security field—alarm systems, cameras, building access systems, and the like—unless you actually work in that specific industry. Security technology is growing so fast that new products are constantly being produced, and the products that are available to you today are really already dated. I have some key contacts in that profession who keep me posted.

Second, no two security situations are quite alike. Human interaction is always dynamic and never static. It is always in flux. Rarely is there a black-and-white solution to an incident; it is almost always gray. Even though I had been doing this for quite a while, I still made mistakes and found challenges in ascertaining what was really going on and picking the best response I could. I could certainly be taken aback by the mental state of some of our "reality-impaired" patrons. Some days I felt as though all I was doing was trying to keep the patients calm.

The one advantage I do have in my attempts to help you over most others in the security field is that I did indeed work on the front line in a library for seventeen years. Within the library system in Charlotte there were twenty-four libraries of all shapes and sizes in all types of areas. Their staffing varied from very large to a single librarian minding the store. In most cases, the library staff also wore the security hat along with their other duties. The point I am trying to make here is that I know exactly what a librarian goes through. I witnessed it firsthand every day.

I wish I could have had the information that I am now sharing with you when I first started working with the public when I was very young. Even though I had dealt with the public for ten years in retail before I stumbled into the security field, many of the principles I work by today would have readily applied, and I would now have more hair.

As you may have guessed from the title of the book, the martial arts have influenced my perspective in interacting with the problem patron. Don't jump to the conclusion that I am talking about *physical* encounters and that my martial ways imply that I think I am some sort of tough guy. It is the *mental* aspect of that discipline that I want you to consider.

In this book, I share with you the basis of everything I know about dealing with all levels and all kinds of people in various security situations. I am rather straightforward and downright blunt at times. I call this, after all, a "real world" guide. I prefer to tell it to you the way it really is versus what you may want to hear. I relate the stories as they happened—colorful, earthy language and all.

The information contained within is simple. There is a great strength in simplicity, but our oh-so-magnificent intellect convinces us that the best solutions are the most complicated, and we sometimes end up outthinking ourselves. Einstein once said that, when you can't find a solution to a problem, you need to go back to the basics. I am reminded of that popular expression these days that tells everyone to "think outside the box," but that presupposes that one can think *inside* the box to start with.

However, *simple* does not always mean *easy*. These tactics that I am providing you take practice, especially if you are passive by nature, which many (but certainly not all) librarians are. I don't mean that in a demeaning way. We are all born passive (as I was) or aggressive by our very nature, and we tend to follow that genetic predisposition throughout our lives. I am going to help you be more assertive if you need to be.

I believe that you have to have a certain level of people skills to be able to keep your sanity when working with the public. Not all patrons are pleasant to deal with, but the problematic patrons are still patrons nonetheless. Every day at the reference desk is not going to be full of moonlight and canoe rides. I am sorry if they failed to teach you in library school that all the nuts aren't in the nuthouse. Some of the librarians I have known don't even like the public, and I have often wondered why in the world they ever became involved in a profession that demands helping people.

The whole idea, and my fervent wish in producing this text, is to empower you to be able to *respond* to a situation rather than simply *react*. Animals react, people should respond. However, since we humans are creatures of emotion as well as logic, we often do something and then think about it rather than the opposite. I show you a way to put a plan of action in place, then you can take the first step in controlling your environment.

After traveling constantly ever since I retired from the library (only stopping for six weeks for the birth of my son) and feeling fulfilled by the overwhelmingly positive response to my presentations, I can say that I definitely made the right decision.

I have enjoyed it so much that I can honestly say I have not worked a day since I left the library. This subject of library security still energizes and fascinates me.

This marks my twenty-second anniversary in the library world. I may not be a librarian, but I think I understand your world quite well. I want you to be safe, and I want to help you see the best way of accomplishing that.

You are a professional librarian. You go the extra mile for the patrons and want them to get the information they are seeking. In turn, you ask only that they treat you in a civil manner and not abuse you. I think that is quite fair enough.

Everywhere I go, I gain a great feeling of efficacy when I can help empower a fellow inhabitant of the Planet Library we share. I will always be thankful for the many new and lasting friends I have made over the years. I sincerely hope this little book helps you through your day.

INMATES RUNNING THE ASYLUM

STORIES FROM THE FRONT TRENCHES

*And we are here as on a darkling plane, swept with confused signals
of struggle and flight, where ignorant armies clash by night.*

—Matthew Arnold

BEFORE WE GET too serious, I start on the lighter side, including a few abbreviated tales from my tenure as a library security manager. I could dedicate the entire book to such stories, but I've just picked a few of the best. Of course, they are all true. Who could make these up?

To begin with, some folks will try to tell you that there is no such thing as a dumb question. Obviously they never worked in a library. The top ten dumbest things I have been asked while standing by the circulation desk:

10. "If it's a cloudy day, will they postpone the eclipse of the sun?"
9. "Do your elevators go upstairs?"
8. "Who was that Wells guy and how did he build that time machine?"
7. "Who didn't sign the Declaration of Independence?"
6. "Can I flex something in here?" (They were actually looking for a fax machine.)
5. "Do you have books on witchcraft? My ex-wife has put a mojo on me and now I can't have sex with my girlfriend and my trailer has been repossessed."
4. "Do you have an Orlando newspaper? They have a bunch of felony warrants out for me there and I want to see if I'm in the paper."
3. "How late can I use the computers after you close?"

2. "There's a sign out there that says 'NO PARKING' in big letters. Can I park there?"
1. "Just where in the hell is uptown Charlotte and where is the damn library?"

During my first week at the library, a woman exited a taxi in front of the library. She said hello to everyone at the front desk and said she was leaving town but wanted to do something for the library. She pulled out a checkbook and wrote us a check for one million dollars. After giving it to the stunned circulation staff, she got back in the taxi, never to be seen again. The check was phony, of course.

Another lady happily greeted me one morning as I opened the front door. She asked me where the closest copier was and I took her to it. She then proceeded to pull off her wig and make a copy of it. She thanked me for my help and left.

I once walked into the bathroom to find a fellow who was at least six foot six standing nude in front of the sink and mirror. Nude, that is, with the exception of one sock, pulled up over his knee. He was busy lathering up his entire body, and he turned toward me with a fierce, confrontational look in his eyes. Knowing he probably had an issue or two, I wanted to approach him as easy as possible and decided to use a little humor. "Hey, my friend," I said smiling, "You've lost a sock, haven't you?" pointing to his bare foot. He looked at me, down at his foot, and then back to me. "Hell, boy," he grumbled, "I just found this one!"

I was standing by the front entrance when a huge, boatlike '72 Buick screeched halfway up onto the sidewalk and slammed on the brakes, almost hitting a prominent "No Parking" sign. The micro-miniskirted driver jumped out, leaving the engine running, and ran past me and up to our typewriter room. The room was windowed, so I could clearly witness the woman pulling out a huge pile of blank business checks and typing frantically. I called the police, and as I was waiting for them to arrive and check things out I got a good look at the woman. *He* was over six feet tall and very slim. His black Tina Turner wig was askew on his head, and his falsies were protruding above his knit top. I don't know where he got a pair of heels to fit his huge, narrow feet, but they must have been a size 18. The police arrived and arrested the fellow, who had just stolen the checks from a car uptown. To this day I have never seen another thief bring so much attention to himself.

One afternoon I was called to the nonfiction reading room to find a man face down on a table in a huge pool of gooey, dark burgundy liquid. The mess covered the four-by-six-foot table and dripped over the sides. My first reaction was that he had hemorrhaged somehow, someway, and that he was DRT (dead right there). The responding medics proved me in error. The man had actually guzzled a half-gallon bottle of wine before coming in and was so drunk that he had thrown it all up as he passed out. The maintenance staff was very excited about having to replace twenty-six carpet squares.

I'll never forget the petite little lady who came out of the bathroom one morning. This was a young woman, probably in her twenties. On every inch of exposed skin, including her face and neck, she had hundreds of tiny, open and bleeding sores. I still have no idea what she was suffering from, but she was obviously very ill. She had taken toilet paper and had pressed it over the sores on her arms. I immediately asked her if I should call a medic, trying to find out if she needed help. In twenty-five years of security work, I have never been cursed at like that. She called me everything, and I do mean everything. Luckily, she said all of it as she was walking out the door, and I never saw her again.

I was once called to the women's restroom by a patron who said something weird was happening in one of the stalls. I walked in and under the stall wall I saw four feet extremely close together. I knocked on the door, and after some hesitation and rapid adjustment of clothing a man and woman came sheepishly walking out. He explained that they were having an affair and that the library was the only place they could meet. She was married and he was an ex-felon on parole. She wailed not unlike someone at a Pentecostal funeral and begged me not to call her husband. He was literally on his knees, pleading with me to not call his parole officer. All this made for quite a scene.

Another memorable restroom moment was when I discovered a huge area of excrement on the floor of a stall, right in front of the toilet bowl. When I returned less than one minute later with a maintenance person, someone was sitting and using that very toilet. He had his legs spread to keep his feet out of the previously mentioned mess.

I was called to the reference area on 9-11-2001, just an hour or so after news broke of the tragedy at the World Trade Center. A seventy-eight-year-old gentleman was fistfighting with a sixty-eight-year-old over a business reference book. They were swinging in slow motion, but both obviously had bad intentions. One had already bitten a chunk out of the other's shoulder. I remember thinking that the whole world must be going crazy that day.

My friend was having one heck of a game. He was obviously at the end of the second half, and winning or losing the game was all on his shoulders. He moved in all directions, constantly dribbling and putting moves on his opponents that left them guarding air. He came down the middle, entered the paint, and dunked home two points. There was only one problem with this scene. He was in the middle of the reference area all alone and had no basketball. I went up and asked him to give me his best forward pass, which he did. I challenged him to take it from me and proceeded in an imaginary dribble to the front door. I then gave him back the "ball" and told him he couldn't play basketball in the library because someone could fall and get hurt. He readily agreed and apologized for not thinking of that himself. He came back the next day just long enough to find me and give me a thumbs up. "The Bobcats [Charlotte's basketball team] picked me up in the first round!" he cheered as he dribbled his imaginary ball out the door. We never saw him again.

A fellow came slowly walking into the library one night. He was looking at the ceiling for the most part, and he caught my attention. He then went by one of the service desks and just stood there, looking straight up. I decided to talk to him, but as I started to go over he moved on to the elevators and went to the second floor. My instinct told me that I needed to go up and check him out. I found him in the men's room, where he had taken six rolls of toilet paper and was proceeding to cram them into the commode with his foot. When I approached him, he stopped and turned and just looked at me. I escorted him to the security office and informed him that I was banning him. The entire time he never changed his blank, calm facial expression and never said a word. It was the first and last time I ever saw him.

One fellow was obviously intoxicated, and I escorted him to the security office. He didn't have any liquor on him, but in his duffel bag I found two huge bottles of mouthwash, one with only a couple of spoonfuls left. I assumed that he had the mouthwash to cover up the booze he must continually have on his breath. Then I noticed the alcohol content of the mouthwash and realized that was how he was obtaining his buzz.

There's the old saying that when you have to go, you have to go. At least that is what the woman told me while she was sitting atop a trash can at two o'clock in the middle of a beautiful day right outside the library. She asked me what someone was supposed do when she couldn't find a restroom uptown. In her frustration, she had dropped her pants and was using the trash can as a toilet. Her "business" was complicated, so she was reading a magazine to pass the time. The police, much to their joy, had to lead her away.

Trapped in the park bench of doom, a man was yelling for someone to help him. He needed all the help he could get. In a park outside the children's room, we had several benches that were four feet long and were capped by circular arm rests that were about eighteen inches in diameter. This fellow had decided to sleep off his intoxicated state by lying lengthwise on the bench. He had put both legs through the far arm rest and somehow, someway, had gotten both of this arms over his head and through the other arm rest. You should see that bench. It was an impossible physical feat, but he had done it. When he awoke, he could not get his arms down and was trapped. By the time I arrived at the request of the children's staff, I found about twenty kids looking out the window in amazement and watching what the man was going to do next. I saw that he was drunk, so I called the police to meet me out in the park. During his struggle to free himself, his pants had dropped down to his lower hips, exposing him to the world and to the kids. As the police arrived, he stated that he had to "take a piss" and that we needed to stand back. With that he relieved himself straight up in the air, not unlike Old Faithful at Yellowstone. We adults didn't care for the show, but the kids got a big kick out of it and were pointing, yelling, and cheering as the police freed the guy and carried him to the police car.

Over the years I have seen people drink all kinds of cologne (the cheaper the better, patrons told me). Glue-sniffing stayed popular as well. I began to notice that our automatic deodorizers were seldom working. Eventually I discovered a fellow huffing one of the cans that he had taken out of the dispenser to get high—so *that* was what was going on.

I was in the process of dealing with a man who had cut into a 1920 newspaper from our stacks. "I just don't understand why you are making such a big deal out of this," he screamed. "The damn paper is almost a hundred years old!"

Enter the master of disguise. A white male, about five foot seven and 250 pounds, was banned from the library for being intoxicated and cursing staff. He was dressed in army green camouflage pants and shirt and was accompanied by his companion, a very short black female who was easily as wide as she was tall, with a hot pink snow parka and wildly splayed-out hair. They were banned from the library, but later that evening he came back with his girlfriend and they were both dressed the same way as earlier, but now he had a ski mask on with only his eyes visible. "You guys are really good," he commented as I led him to the security office. "How did you recognize me with my mask on?"

While walking through the Popular selection area I noticed a woman sitting and reading quietly at a back table. Something caught my attention, although at first I didn't know what it was. As I stepped over, I noticed the lady had a huge rat on her shoulder. For a moment I thought she was being attacked by the thing, but as I started to say something I saw her pass a piece of cracker to it. I then saw that the rat had a string around its neck and the other end was attached to the lady's wrist. I can't describe the conversation we had because it made no sense whatsoever. Let's just say that she could not understand why she couldn't have her pet rat Mickey in the library, and I eventually had to have the police help me escort her out and ban her.

A fellow was in the administrative office demanding years of back rent from the library. He stated that he had the original lease he and Andrew Carnegie had agreed on and that he was owed millions of dollars. I told him he would have to return with someone from the Carnegie family, which he readily agreed to and said that would be no problem. The last I saw of him was when he rode away on his little pink girl's bike.

Every once in a while I got a reminder that I never know who I might be dealing with and that no one is necessarily harmless, no matter how they look. A police officer was placing a seemingly hapless gentleman under arrest, and I was helping the officer search the man's pockets. In every pocket of his pants, jacket, and shirt—even in his shirt breast pocket, we found some type of weapon. He had several box cutters, knives, and even a sharpened screwdriver—a total of fourteen weapons. I couldn't resist the temptation to ask him if he was some type of ninja.

I literally saved a pervert from his victim one morning. He had exposed himself to her in the stacks, and she really got upset. He actually came to me for help. I had more trouble keeping her away from him than I did actually banning him. "Go ahead!" he begged me. "Take my damn picture so I can get out of here!"

Okay, before you ask me for another top ten list, here you go—compiled by my security officers and me over the years in a sometimes desperate attempt to find the humor in the midst of what could be very serious duties. These are the most rejected library marketing phrases:

The Public Library . . .

> . . . Where the Possessed Go to Mingle!
> . . . A House of Knowledge. Do You Fit?
> . . . Patron Dress Code: Four Tooth Minimum
> . . . Don't Force Us to Call the Circus!
> . . . Where There IS Such a Thing as a Stupid Question
> . . . No, Our Staff Members Do Not Want to Date You
> . . . Where the Demons Go to Hang Out
> . . . All the Nuts Are Not in the Nuthouse
> . . . Yes, We Are a Public Building, but No, You Can't Do Anything You Want

2

DEMYSTIFYING THE CONCEPT OF A SECURITY PROGRAM

TWELVE ESSENTIAL ELEMENTS OF REAL-WORLD LIBRARY SECURITY

The answer is in the simple, but is sought in the far away.

—Mencius

I WRITE A great deal about simplicity in his book. There is a great strength in simplicity, but it is so very hard to convey at times, even to ourselves. We are oh-so-intellectual after all. Answers, we say, just can't be that simple.

But that is exactly what you should constantly strive for in the development of your security program. And after you complete it, always review it on a regular basis to winnow out anything that proves to be unnecessary.

I would also add that a firm commitment to controlling the library environment is absolutely essential. In other words, consistency, consistency, consistency. I have certainly visited libraries that simply do not put up with disruptive behavior, and it is the staff who make sure of that. I have also seen libraries in the same system—just a few miles apart—where one branch is on top of things and another is seemingly oblivious to everything happening around it and avoiding contact with the patrons if at all possible.

I know that it sounds good to say that you don't want to "confront patrons" about their behavior and that you don't want to be a "house of correction," and that you want everyone to have a "great library experience" and have a place where patrons can "be themselves," and so on. I too wanted to teach the world to sing in perfect harmony. But then you have the guy who follows an employee through the staff door a half hour before you open, goes to a computer, and logs on, knowing full well what he is doing. You approach him and he ignores you or goes off the deep end, maybe even so far as to curse or threaten you. What do you do with *him*?

Your plan should aid you in sustaining an environment that is conducive to library use. Period. Look at your existing plan. Does it help you, hinder you, or not actually say anything? Or does it attempt to say too much? In that case you have to be careful that you do not make staff too dependent on the manual. Enable staff to use their discretion when needed.

Frontline staff need help. They do not have the support staff or the time to keep up some complex system and vacuous procedures with multiple warnings.

In my experiences both with the public library in Charlotte and during my extensive consulting travels, I see the same repeated issues. In my opinion, there are twelve fundamentals you must take into consideration to have a truly effective security and safety program. You don't need to meet all of them to make progress, but if you leave any out, your procedures will be lacking.

1. Establish sound rules for the use of the library and guidelines for their enforcement.
2. Recognize dangerous assumptions.
3. Treat everyone the same.
4. Be consistent.
5. Develop and maintain realistic awareness.
6. Use simple documentation.
7. Establish regular training.
8. Have control of all keys.
9. Review all procedures periodically.
10. Use a security checklist.
11. Develop outside relationships.
12. Have simple emergency plans.

1. ESTABLISH RULES AND GUIDELINES

You must set established rules and regulations for library use. Although *most* rules in libraries I have seen are for the *most* part common sense, as Voltaire put it best, "Common sense is not so common."

I am often asked how best to express rules, and this question usually comes from a desire to state rules in a welcoming way. Well, of course you want patrons to come in and enjoy the library. But just remember that the most unwelcoming thing is a chaotic environment, and keep the wording simple and direct. Don't say with thirty words what you can state with five.

Here's an example. If your library does not allow cell phones, put up a sign that says: "Welcome to you library. For everyone's comfort during your visit, would you please silence your cell phone. Thank you and have a wonderful day!" Try that one for about three months, then replace it with a sign that simply says, "No cell phones."

The sound of the first, soft version is well intentioned, but it is better and far more effective to use the second, direct manner. Try both examples and you will see that the second version is much more effective than asking patrons to "please" do something. When you start the rule like that, it sounds like a request rather than a statement of something that is not allowed.

Making sure your staff is consistent is a much higher priority and will get you quicker results than endlessly debating how to word the rules. I have found that the patrons who need to be told the rules the most need to see them in the simplest and frankest manner possible.

Another popular theory is to not tell the patrons what they cannot do and instead focus on what they can do. Brother! Please get on with communicating in a straightforward manner with the problem patron. Sooner or later it all comes down to "no," whether you want to admit it to yourself or not.

The rules also have to be clear and concise so you can interpret them with confidence in the midst of a security incident. When everything is hitting the fan, you have no time to dig through some nebulous policy, trying to figure out if a rule applies to the situation and to what extent.

My favorite story about unnecessary verbiage comes from the days of World War II. A civil defense pamphlet issued by the government stated, "Illumination must be extinguished when this premises is vacated." Upon seeing this, President Roosevelt became aggravated and said, "Damn! Why can't they just say turn out the lights when you leave the house?"

And please do away with any nonsensical rules. I always disliked many of the rules in Charlotte that the board of trustees and our lawyer had decided upon. I thought some of them were unnecessary and others far too wordy. One in particular forbade "soliciting for prostitution." Wow, where does it say I can't be a hooker in here?

And do you really need to state that you cannot steal from the library? With regard to rules, it should always be about less and not more. I have seen many bizarre rules in my travels, but stating that patrons can't steal always surprises me.

A rule against "causing intentional alarm by indecent exposure" was another great one I saw during my travels. "Well," I suppose the perpetrator would say, "I didn't *intend* to alarm her; it was just my way of saying hello!"

One rule you should have for sure is a little jewel I came up with several years after I began working at the library. I have since shared this many times with other libraries, and they now consistently use it. Simply put, it forbids "any behavior that is disruptive to library use."

Let me illustrate why this is so great to have in writing as part of your rules and regulations for library use. When writing rules, you might find it impossible to define exactly what "someone smelling bad" or "having an offensive odor" means. Nevertheless, you know that a patron who clears out the entire nonfiction area when she enters it smells bad. If you can smell someone from fifteen feet away, that patron is certainly displaying behavior "disruptive to library use."

The same applies to the patron who wants to stand at the circulation desk and argue endlessly about fines or some other problem. At times the matter at hand is a dead issue, since you have given this patron breaks before or this is a time when no possible exception can be made. You do not have time to keep listening and saying the same thing in reply over and over. Past a certain point, such a patron has become too "disruptive to library use," because you have other patrons to help or other duties to complete.

The library needs to know exactly what it wants to be to the public and realize the inherent limitations. The libraries that try to be everything to everyone and always say yes to the patron are often the ones that have the most problems.

Again, your rules should be as simple and brief as possible. You should be able to put them on a large, bookmark-sized card, as in figure 2.1. When you change your rules or go to this format, always include one of these bookmarks for every patron when they check materials out. Have a stack of these cards at the self-checkout station for patrons as well.

The rules suggested in figure 2.1 are given only as examples, and I don't mean to imply that they are applicable to your particular library. Only you can ultimately decide upon the rules you need, because you are the one who actually works in your library. No one but you can know your clientele and what rules are necessary to control the environment. The location of your library and your usual patrons dictate the rules you need.

Once you have the rules set, you must develop guidelines. Here's what I mean. Say you do not allow sleeping. How many times do you wake someone up before there is a consequence? You might decide that you should wake someone twice, then the third time he is asleep he has to leave for the day. This way, you don't have staff members giving out different numbers of warnings, which could imply bias. Lack of guidelines can lead to bias—even if it is innocent bias—since there is no structure, so take away the mystery for the staff. With guidelines, everyone can be on the same page, so to speak, and therefore be consistent in informing patrons of the rules.

Then there is another threshold in the guidelines. What if you are always putting someone out for the day? Do you have the time to deal with the same folks over and over? Your guideline might be that after they are ejected for the day three times, the next time means they are out for three months or six months—however you want to structure it.

Keep the ban periods to just three or four stages at the most. But you must establish them so the staff will not have different interpretations. If you have too many levels, such as one week, one month, three months, six months, one year, and five years (yes, I have seen such a policy), you just end up confusing your staff and managers. They cannot keep up with such a complicated policy.

Loitering is another issue I am constantly asked about. Although most libraries have a rule against loitering, very few can actually tell me what "loitering" means to their library. Here is the bottom line based

We want your visit to be a pleasant one. Use of the library is intended to be for reading, research, studying, and learning. Other use is not permitted.

The library does not allow:

* Any behavior that is disruptive to library use.
* Sleeping
* Loitering
* Food or drink
* Soliciting or selling
* Misuse of restrooms
* Not wearing shoes or shirt
* Petitioning/distributing materials
* Excessive number or size bags
* Leaving children under the age of 8 unattended by a responsible person of at least 16 years of age.

The library is a public building. Please do not to leave your children unattended!

Theft or damage of library materials is a serious offense and may lead to arrest.

Failure to comply with the library may result in suspension of library privileges.

Trespassers will be prosecuted.

FIGURE 2.1

on my observations: People in the library should be using the library. If you let people just come in and hang out for whatever reason, it lends itself to behavior problems. I have found that, overall, libraries that require you to be reading, studying, and the like have much more control over their environment than the ones that allow someone to come in and stare at the ceiling all day as long as they are "not bothering anyone."

Many times in my travels frustrated staff members tell me that their library is trying to be everything to everyone, living the fantasy of always having "win-win" situations where you never have to say no to anyone. But the plain fact is that people cannot do whatever they want in your building, so that requires you to educate patrons as to what you do not allow, and *there is no getting around that fact*. It is as simple as this:

> You have rules for library use.
>
> Patrons must follow those rules.
>
> If they don't, they can't use the library.

A critical point: the library administration has to know what it wants to accomplish with the security program, and you need to know that the administration is going to back you up once you advise someone of policy. Everyone has to be on the same page. You simply cannot have priorities that the administration does not have, and the administration cannot expect you to follow procedures if it overturns your frontline decision each time a patron complains.

Once the library develops its rules, it must then establish who is to advise the patron of those rules. Can part-time pages tell a patron he can't have food and drink in the library, or must pages always report rule infractions to a full-time employee? Or you do allow only managers to advise patrons of rules? If you have security, at what point do they step in?

So, keep your rules simple and clarify your guidelines. Make sure the staff know the rules (you would be amazed at the libraries I have visited where many staff simply do not know what is not allowed in their own building), and make the decision to move ahead with it all. Don't get bogged down trying to create a perfect policy. There is no such thing, and when you discover weaknesses in your procedures you will adjust them. After all, security is a living thing and doesn't remain fixed. If you are not careful, you can end up with policy that is so wishy-washy it doesn't really say anything.

2. RECOGNIZE DANGEROUS ASSUMPTIONS

Don't allow yourself to become complacent. Vow never to say these five things again, because they can put you in harm's way sooner or later:

"He's harmless." Very few human beings are completely harmless under the right circumstances. What a silly thing to say when it comes to your safety.

"He has never been a problem before." The news is full of first-time criminals. Maybe you are just on borrowed time, my friend.

"We have never had a problem before." Maybe (and probably), you've just been lucky. If there is one village idiot, he *will* find his way to the library sooner or later. There are patrons who will take advantage of your security vulnerabilities. Usually the staff who are most insistent about saying this are the most clueless about what is going on right under their noses.

"We have always done it that way." That doesn't mean you are doing it right or the best way to help keep you safe.

"Other libraries do it that way." That doesn't mean they know what is best for you (or even for them, for that matter). Think for yourselves. One of the worst things you can do is to copy someone else's procedures blindly without fully understanding your library's issues and applying what sometimes are solutions unique to your building.

3. TREAT EVERYONE THE SAME

When advising patrons of rules, you must always go by their behavior and never their appearance. You must have the same consequences for everyone no matter what their station in life appears to be. Having rules is not a problem, but if you pick and choose who to enforce the rules with, that will get you into trouble quickly. Treat everyone the same and you won't have to work in fear of being accused of bias. Those accusations always come, but your documentation will show that you take problem patrons as they come.

I refer to all the folks I have to deal with as "behavior problems." We never call them anything that could make us sound biased in any way, so please forget terms like "street people," "yuppies from hell," or "Satan's spawn." Yes, I have heard those things said by staff during my visits to libraries. Please remember: you are behind a reference desk, not in a soundproof booth.

4. BE CONSISTENT

You have to be consistent in enforcement. This is such a huge priority. How many times has a patron said to you, "Well, they let me do this yesterday"? Please make it a priority with staff to be on the same page and to make everyone's job (including their own) easier by being consistent when informing patrons about what is not allowed. Once you set the new standard, you have to stay on top of it each day. What conduct is going to lead to being banned and for how long? What conduct will lead to detention for arrest and how? What offenses will lead to prosecution? These are all things to consider before you start a new program.

5. DEVELOP AND MAINTAIN REALISTIC AWARENESS

You must control your environment through your constant awareness. Awareness is *the* key element to protecting yourself anywhere you are, and that certainly includes the workplace. Practice cultivating your awareness of what is going on around you, and soon it will become second nature. You can do this without becoming paranoid, and in a short time you develop a kind of sixth sense.

During my retail years I could tell you immediately when a potential shoplifter came into the store. Similarly, aspiring lawbreakers have also developed a sense of when someone has recognized that they may have bad intentions. They want to go about their "business" in stealth, and your awareness may be all it takes to dissuade them.

Work on what I like to call your quiet awareness by practicing "30-30-30." This means for the next thirty days you are going to stop whatever you are doing every thirty minutes and look around for thirty seconds. Observe who you can and what they are doing from your vantage point on the thirty-minute mark. Do not go looking for someone to observe. Really pause, concentrate for the thirty seconds, and look. Do this for a month, and not only will you start seeing the overt things that may have been always happening around you, but you will also develop a tangible feeling when something is not quite right. You need to heed such feelings.

This intuition is given to us by nature, but as spoiled Americans living in a relatively safe society our guard has been lowered over the years. If you work in a public entity like a library these days, you'd best get it back.

6. USE SIMPLE DOCUMENTATION

Document all security incidents. This is absolutely essential not only for the administration but for possible future reference. If, for instance, you ban someone and she someday returns, you will not be able to have her arrested or prosecute her for trespassing if you cannot show the precise who, when, and why of the ban.

You may also need to document every time you correct patron behavior to show how busy you are in your security endeavors. We all know that the day is long gone when we can go to our administrators and say, "Gee, we sure are busy down front, and we have to talk to people all day about the rules" and expect to get the help you need.

You can also record and keep track of your potential problems, including those patrons who may be establishing some pattern of wrongful behavior, as well as that guy who always seems to be staring at you and giving you the creeps. By documenting, you have all the information you need for banning if that is what some behavior leads to. I have some forms to help you with this in chapter 7.

7. ESTABLISH REGULAR TRAINING

You must establish a system to train all employees. You don't go into a lion cage with a book on lion taming. Everyone needs to know security and safety procedures up front, what is expected of them and *that they will be held accountable when they do not follow through*. They need to understand that security is part of everyone's job, and that one person not doing her part can collapse all the safeguards that have been put in place. We need to avoid this: "Hey, I thought that *you* locked the front door last night before we left!"

I hate to even use the phrase *everyone's job*, because this goes beyond job description. It's just part of life, really. It's bigger than your "job." It's about your safety and well-being.

Training classes can be based on any number of things. You need a basic orientation for your new staff members, and you need a review class everyone must attend annually. You should always incorporate security as part of any monthly or bimonthly meetings you have with staff.

Ask yourself right now: How many of my staff know what to do in an emergency? Do they know clear procedures to protect themselves? Do they even know the existing rules of the library? Do you think that just because you have posted rules, your staff will read and understand them on their own? You are making a huge mistake if you take anyone's training for granted. Break it all down to its most elemental level. Never assume your staff knows anything on their own. Oh, the stories I could tell of staff who were constantly complaining about their security but had no clue as to what procedures already existed for their safety.

You can use role-playing or "synthetic training" sessions, which I think are some of the very best ways for everyone to get into the rhythm of patron interaction. Perform the exercises when the building is closed so you can actually execute in various areas where problems might occur, like the circulation desk. You need to make it as real as possible. This technique makes a huge difference over just training in a meeting room.

All staff can take turns being disagreeable patrons and agreeable actors, and you just set up an assortment of scenarios based on things that have actually happened. After a little initial nervousness, passive staff members come to see how much better they are than they expected, and they are amazed at how some of the more aggressive folks flub everything up, which gives them even more confidence. Just be careful not to put two employees together who don't especially care for each other. Here are some scenarios you could use:

What would you do if . . .

> a patron slammed his hand on the counter and said, "I'm sick and tired of the library's poor service!"
>
> someone was asleep on a newspaper that a patron needed to use
>
> a patron had his shirt off and was bathing in the bathroom
>
> a patron cursed at you then immediately said, "I'm so sorry. I've had a terrible week! If one more thing goes wrong! Please forgive me!"
>
> after you corrected a teenager, he said, "Go shelve a book, you stupid librarian!"
>
> a student came up to you and said, "I can't study over there. That woman who came to sit at my table stinks like hell!"
>
> a very upset patron told you, "I can't even use this library. That guy keeps trying to talk to me, and no matter how many times I tell him I'm trying to read, he keeps bothering me!"

You can see all the areas you can explore. Plan this type of training after you share the information in chapter 5, and you will be surprised at how much staff enjoy it and how much everyone gains.

8. HAVE CONTROL OF ALL KEYS

You must establish a key control system. If you can't tell me who has ever had a key of some type to your building and where that key is now, you need to rekey your building. Period.

This is not nearly as complicated as it may seem, and it doesn't have to be expensive—that is, if you know what you want and how to plan it, instead of relying on most keysmiths, who make more money the more keys they sell you.

It breaks down like this: You will have master, area master, and individual door keys. If you have pages who need access only to the book drop area, they have that one door (or bin) key. Do they also need to use the employee entrance? Fine, they get a key to that one door as well. The idea is that precious few have a master to every area in the building. Do your children's staff all need access to every door in that specific area? Then you can issue an area master to each of them.

Letter and number the keys by having the locksmith stamp them "M" for master, "AM" for area master, and "D" for door. If you have five master keys made, stamp them "M-1," "M-2," "M-3," and so on. The children's area master can be stamped "AM-1-#1," "AM-1-#2," "AM-1-#3," and so on. If you also have a genealogical section that needs an area master, stamp that one "AM-2-#1." Your circulation area could be "AM-3-#1." Mark individual door keys using the same method.

Place one key in a locked key box installed in the manager's office. Only the manager and the assistant have access. Repeat after me, please: only the manager and the assistant have access. If everyone can get into the key box, you soon have keys lost or mishandled, and no one wants to admit to losing them. If someone loses keys, they pay at least $10 per key, and you may want to consider a higher cost for losing master keys.

Simply make up a list of your numbered keys on your computer, the dates they were issued, and who obtained them. Now if a staff member loses his keys, you can immediately check to see what keys you issued him and what areas of the library have been made vulnerable; do any locks now need to be rekeyed?

9. REVIEW ALL PROCEDURES PERIODICALLY

You must review your procedures periodically because your vulnerabilities change. Troublemakers can, and often do, find ways to circumvent your security procedures. At least annually, management should sit down and take a hard, honest look at existing procedures and determine how they need to be updated and improved.

10. USE A SECURITY CHECKLIST

You need to develop a security checklist to be used by all your branches on a monthly basis. You can include things such as these:

first-aid kit stocked

outside lights all working

extra keys secured and accounted for

new staff have received security training

snow melter in good condition

emergency numbers updated

fire extinguishers charged

emergency exits clear

emergency lighting working properly

security manuals in place at each public service desk

maintenance areas clean and orderly to OSHA specifications

You see what I mean. Include any items or areas that pertain specifically to safety and security. This monthly review is vital no matter the size of your building or the level of your problems. It ensures that safety procedures are on a level equal to any other statistics or procedures you follow.

11. DEVELOP OUTSIDE RELATIONSHIPS

You must develop relationships with the police, social services, and local schools. If I were a branch manager, I would meet with the local police to tell them what happens in libraries and to let them know that we have security procedures, that everyone on my staff is trained, and that we are certainly not going to call the police unless we need them. In other words, if we call, it's serious business—so get here as quickly as you can.

I had contacts with social services for adults and children. Kids with lice? I called my source for help. An adult with obvious mental problems that looked like he needed assistance? Ditto.

I had many indigent patrons, so you can bet I knew everyone who worked at the homeless shelter. They knew we treated everyone the same and that everyone was welcome in the library as long as they followed the rules. This connection kept us out of a lot of possible trouble.

Is your branch close to a school? Maybe a contact can help you disseminate information to the students about what you do not allow in the public library. Such a source can also prove valuable when you are trying to identify problem students.

12. HAVE SIMPLE EMERGENCY PLANS

You need to develop simple emergency plans for your building in case of fire, severe weather, medical situation, or bomb threat. How do you evacuate the building, and where does everyone meet outside? How do you notify the fire department? Who notifies the patrons, and how do you search for those still inside the building? If you have a monitored fire system and paging capabilities, it makes things easier, but staff still need the training in conjunction with the technology.

Where do you gather inside if you have a tornado warning? Do you have a weather radio to monitor conditions? Meet with your local fire department and have them come to your library to help you.

If you have a medical situation, who calls 911 and what do they say? Who meets the responders at the front door? How do you get them to the person who needs them?

BE HONEST IN your assessment of your building needs. Hoping problems will go away by ignoring them or wishing you will never have them is not the path to take. Be proactive and make whatever changes you can. Get several staff members together and give them the assignment of thinking like a group of problem patrons. Have them go over your building inside and out, and task them to discover the vulnerable areas. You don't need a fancy form, just a few sheets of paper. You may be surprised to see what they find.

Now ask yourself . . .

In which of these aspects are you lacking?

Do you have guidelines for your rules?

Do you treat everyone the same?

What are the weaknesses of your current plan?

3

THE LIBRARIAN IN THE MIRROR

Truth cannot be perceived until we come to understand ourselves.

—Bruce Lee

FOR THOSE OF you who say to yourselves that you just can't step up and tell a patron that he can't do something, or that you can't do what needs to be done in an expedient manner, I tell you this: the subconscious has no sense of humor whatsoever. Every single cell in your body is listening to you constantly and hears you tell yourself that you can or cannot do this or that. How you talk to yourself is a personal journey indeed, and though others can help you, ultimately only you can know what makes you tick. I can't do that for you.

If I could learn to be security conscious, anyone can, and I could not be more sincere when I say that. During my seminars when I say that by nature I am passive, introverted, and emotional, many people look at me like I'm being coy just to give them a false sense of confidence. But that is simply not true. Why would I try to mislead you on this when I'm trying to help you? I assure you that my sense of confidence in this area was hard fought and hard won.

Some may say that it is easier for me because I am a man. Women, are you hearing yourselves? Please! I have taught these techniques to thousands of female library staff and security personnel, and gender often works in your favor rather than hampering you. Or people assume I have military experience that helps me have the proper bearing; sorry to disappoint, but I was never in the service. I try to stay in reasonable shape, so some say that makes the difference. And though I believe that it doesn't hurt, especially for a security officer, I have seen folks of all shapes and sizes who can project authority. These are skills anyone can learn if they simply *work* to apply them.

FINDING YOUR PERSONAL RHYTHM: FIVE QUESTIONS TO ASK YOURSELF

I like to quote Lord Byron, who once wrote that "adversity is the first path to truth." How very true that is. When we face a challenging situation, such as an unruly patron, we quickly find out how much confidence we have under pressure.

This subject alone could fill a book. I will just say that, first, we must have a *willingness to engage* the patron. We must have the desire to acquire and hone our skill level in this regard. You can have the propensity to be unnerved by the public, or even be just plain afraid of patrons, and still develop an adequate skill level. But you have to apply yourself and be honest with yourself regarding your weaknesses. After all, you can't "get a hold of yourself" if you don't know what to grab onto. *An ability to develop interpersonal skills starts with first developing and maintaining an inner compatibility.*

I would wager that most people have no idea why in some situations they react without thinking, while in other circumstances they think and respond clearly. When you have to ask yourself, "What was I thinking?" more than likely you weren't thinking at all.

You don't want to be a human *doing* rather than a human *being*. Do you want to be a sum total of your fear that marches to the rhythm of whatever is happening around you, or a being who is aware of, understands, and flows with your personal, natural, inner rhythm?

If you have difficulties in this area, the following exercise will help you. Anyone who works with the public should ask themselves five basic questions and take the time to answer them honestly:

AM I INTROVERTED OR EXTROVERTED?

Nothing wrong with being introverted, but you are in a people business, after all. The more willingness to engage patrons you develop, the more it helps you on multiple levels.

If you are more extroverted, please remember that there is sometimes a point in a discussion with patrons when you need to back off and let them do the talking. Most assertive people I know need to spend a little more time really listening. Are you really hearing the patron or just waiting for a chance to talk?

AM I PASSIVE OR AGGRESSIVE?

Neither of these is bad, but you should understand how you are naturally inclined. If you are more often passive by nature, remember that you are sometimes going to have to go against the grain to be able to step up and take action in a tense situation.

If you tend to be aggressive, you need to remind yourself often to pull back on the reins, so to speak. You simply cannot say everything that naturally pops into your head. Please measure your thoughts before you speak.

AM I MORE EMOTIONAL OR MORE OF A LOGIC-BASED THINKER?

Most of us are emotional; it's part of the human condition. Early trauma that some of us experienced as kids left us with an even greater proclivity for emotional reactions. Just remember that you need to guard yourself from knee-jerk or overreactions in time of stress.

If you tend to be a more cool-headed thinker, please keep in mind that there is a time to make a decision and go with it. I admire people who have that natural ability to keep their head on straight amid chaos, but sometimes they suffer from "paralysis by analysis" and cannot decide what to do.

Emotions often guide us more than we care to admit, and it's surprising how many are completely unaware of their overall effect. As I mentioned in the introduction, emotional thinking is the main reason we tend to *react* rather than *respond*.

DO I LIKE PEOPLE?

Why in the world would anyone who does not like people want to work in a library? I have never understood that. You are in a people business, and patrons want and expect a level of competent, pleasant service. You can still provide this if you don't like them, but it is going to take more effort from you to put aside how you really feel, so watch it.

DO I LIKE MY JOB?

I know the feeling you get when you are working a job that you feel is a dead end or one that you just do not like. But if you cannot put those feelings in their place and keep them from affecting how you treat patrons, *you* can end up being the behavior problem—not the patron.

A SELF-SUPPORT SYSTEM:
THREE VITAL ACES TO KEEP UP YOUR SLEEVE

I kept a little sign in my office near the door so that I *had* to look at it every time I exited my office. I just printed it on my computer. All it said was "A.A.A." There were no fancy borders, and it was not on parchment or colored paper. It wasn't there to impress or to look good. It was my reminder that Warren needs to keep his head on straight today at work—a simple reminder of something that is hard to accomplish at times.

When you deal with an upset patron, the last thing you want to do is make the situation worse by your own actions. That happens a great deal more than some care to think about. We have all worked with people who never will admit when they are wrong, and it can be maddening. But how often do we take a real look at our own behavior and have the courage to see the error in our own ways?

Some of us have a more natural ability to be happy, content, and confident than others. Nothing seems to bother some folks, and they maintain a pleasant countenance. They are human like the rest of us, but they are blessed with an even and positive temperament. But many of us are just not that way. We tend to be a little more mercurial in our conduct. We go through cyclical highs and lows to varying degrees. I blame it on whoever came up with that damn yin/yang thing (yes, that's a joke). We have a bad day, and it usually shows. How can you go about not letting one problem create another? The answer is that you must have an effective self-support system of some type, and to do that you have to know what really makes you tick. How can you have a positive effect on the patron if you can't have one on yourself?

So, back to my little A.A.A. sign, which was such an important part of *my* self-support system. It stands for *attitude, approach,* and *analysis.*

ATTITUDE

Simply put, what is your frame of mind as you enter your workplace? Are you having a good day or a bad one? What personal problems are eating at you? Car trouble? Family illness? Did the dog ruin the carpet last night? Or are you having work-related problems? Do you want to make your boss disappear? Is your coworker sending you to an early grave? Still fuming about that last work review? Or maybe you just don't feel like being at work today. There are quite a few mornings when I would simply like to stay in bed.

There are many things that can be troubling us. We all carry burdens. The trick is to develop ways to put them on a back burner while you are at work and to not allow these problems to create other problems with patrons. Personnel manuals universally demand we not bring personal problems or feelings to the workplace. I'd like to ask the author of such instruction if I can visit them sometime in never-never land.

Early on in my martial arts experience, I found that it was easier to control another person than to control myself. My instructor would talk of *mizo no kokoro,* a "mind like water." You have to keep your mind calm and focused, he said, like a calm body of water, to accurately reflect the world around you. Negative emotions are like ripples in the water, distorting the reflection. It's such a sweet little analogy, but it's so very difficult some days.

APPROACH

What is the best way to approach *this* particular situation right now? How can I de-escalate the situation instead of making it worse? Remember what I said earlier about solutions often not being simply black-and-white, but many times gray. Interactions with the public often demand much discretion. Contrary to popular belief, employees *are* paid to think. If your attitude is straight and your head clear, you can come up with a reasonable course of action.

Here's an example. Let's say a man comes to the circulation desk, tosses some DVDs on the counter, smiles as he leans toward you, and slurs, "Check these out for me, honey." His breath parts your hair. His eyes look like two tomatoes in a glass of buttermilk. Yes, he is blasted.

Your security procedures may require you to call the police or security if you encounter someone who is intoxicated. But what would you do now? Would you call for help, or would you quickly check out the materials and get him out the door? See my point?

I tried my best to work with problem patrons. Telling people no carried its hazards, and I was well aware of them. I gave such folks as much latitude as their behavior would allow me to. If you think I just looked for trouble and was just itching to tell patrons to leave, that's about the same as calling me crazy.

ANALYSIS

After an incident, it is paramount that you ask, of both yourself and your staff, which tactics worked and which ones failed. What could you have done differently to affect the outcome?

If you think developing your attitude and approach is challenging, you haven't seen anything until you get employees in a meeting analyzing a security incident and trying to get anyone to admit they blew it. Some employees hate to admit when they are wrong and get a little uptight and defensive. Often they sit and struggle to rationalize their actions, putting more stress on themselves than if they just said they could have handled it better. Try to put them at ease. Show that you are doing this to help them. The purpose is not to criticize but to work through the incident as a team.

Of course, you want to revisit things not only when they go wrong but when they go smoothly. Share the successful tactics with the staff not present at the time of the incident. The bottom line is to learn from everyone's mistakes as well as their triumphs. Sooner or later, everyone has to deal with a behavior problem. Ultimately you are doing all of this for a safer workplace and greater peace of mind.

Exploring and working earnestly within these three areas will do much to improve your staff working together to make security incidents and their aftermath a great deal easier to live with.

Now ask yourself . . .

> How aware are you of your own thinking process while at work?
>
> Are you helping or hindering yourself by the way you think?
>
> How honest are you with yourself regarding how you handle security situations or irate patrons?

4

THE TAO OF "NO"

If I had six hours to chop down a tree, I'd spend five of them sharpening my axe.

—Abraham Lincoln

ALL RIGHT, HERE we go. Once you have your security program in place, including a nice little list of rules to help you control the conduct of your visitors, how in the world do you go up to a perfect stranger and tell her she can't be doing what she is doing? What do you say to best ensure her compliance? And, most important, how do you accomplish this in the safest way possible?

One thing to keep in mind is that telling someone that she cannot do something is not synonymous with a "confrontation." If you feel that way when you approach someone, you are putting way too much stress upon yourself. It is all in the "communication." Watch that self-talk.

APPROACHING PATRONS WHO ARE NOT FOLLOWING RULES OF CONDUCT

I told folks no for quite a long time. I certainly had my share of challenges and, trust me, I learned much the hard way. Here are some universal guidelines to help the process go smoothly for you. I used them every day.

Always approach patrons with the attitude that they will comply and that this is not going to be a big deal. Most of your patrons will listen to you and correct their behavior if you walk up to them with an easy manner and know what you're doing.

They either know better in the first place, are continuing with their behavior until someone tells them to stop, or simply don't realize they are doing something wrong and will readily go along with you.

You can start off nice and then get more authoritative if you need to, but you can't do the opposite. If you come on too strong, you can easily embarrass someone into a verbal or even physical confrontation, especially if they are with someone else or in a group—so watch your tone of voice. Even the look on your face can make a difference, since you start communicating with your expression before you even open your mouth. So if you're having a bad day, relax your mug before you walk up to a patron and try to correct his behavior.

Two phrases I used constantly were "I know you didn't know, but . . ." and "I know there isn't a [or you didn't see the] sign, but . . . ." By approaching patrons this way you are giving them an out and putting them at ease. They usually don't feel the need to get defensive with you. The last thing you want them to think is that you think they are idiotic for their behavior (even though sometimes they are).

If you tend to gesticulate, always use palms-up, openhanded gestures. Never point your finger at anyone and never, ever touch them. Remember to not get too close to them. Everyone has a comfort zone from which they like to communicate. Personal space begins at about twenty inches for most people. Disturbed or upset people are even more sensitive about their private space, so be careful and give everyone some distance.

Even though you should approach confidently, you also need to exercise a sense of due caution because, after all, you usually don't know the person, and who knows what's really going on between their ears. Try to keep a table or chair between you. Maintain a barrier if at all possible. Don't automatically go around and get beside them.

It is also very important to never turn your back on a patron whose behavior you have just corrected. I know of situations where patrons seemed to comply, then verbally, or at times physically, assaulted the employee when his back was turned. Keep the patron in your sight at least peripherally until you are a safe distance away. This takes a little practice, but watching a patron in a discreet way can be done. Remember that aggression is a survival instinct, and there are some freaked-out people out there who are waiting for just one more person to tell them no.

I want to impress upon you how absolutely deceiving appearances can be. They are no reflection on how someone is going to react to you. Some of the toughest, meanest, most destitute-looking people have been the first to comply; often the most professional-appearing can catch you unaware and be the biggest jerks.

If the patron is obviously under the influence of drugs or alcohol, call 911 or your security immediately. I am not talking about patrons with a faint smell of booze on their breath; I am talking about patrons who can hardly articulate or are stumbling around—in other words, a patron any reasonable person would agree is blasted or wigged-out on some controlled substance. I discuss such out-of-control behavior in chapter 5.

As best you can, be deaf to insulting language directed at you (more on this in chapter 5). Experienced behavior problems know that by upsetting you they can use your emotions against you and control you.

Never argue with a behavior problem. Most are quite experienced at pointless argument, and you seldom win. Many patrons have a PhD in "why," knowing that why can be an endless, open question. And some people on the street survive by talking—you can't outtalk them—so don't get caught up in a no-win situation. Tell them what you can or cannot do for them in a polite, clear, concise, and direct way, then move on.

Be prepared to be accused of some type of prejudice. Behavior problems sometimes say that you are just doing this to them because of their race, their age, their monetary status or lack thereof, or the part of the country they are from; I've heard them all. One lady told me I was banning her not because she was concealing fourteen paperbacks and trying to get past the book alarm but because "she was a Christian." As if I would know that.

They may be accusing you of being biased because of past wrongs in their life, but often they just want to put you on the defensive. Don't fall for this ploy. Stay with the real issue at hand. If you treat everyone the same and go by their behavior, not appearance, then you don't have to live in fear of such accusations.

Remember that suspicion and guilt are two different things. Be 110 percent sure you have the right person and not just 99 percent. If you approach patrons and you are not sure what is going on, give them the benefit of the doubt until you do. This is another reason an easy and soft approach is so vital.

DEALING WITH TEENS AND CHILDREN

First, a few words about the teens. This age group seems to be a growing problem in libraries, but I think the strategy for effectively dealing with it is pretty straightforward. I am hardly a child psychologist, and certainly not a teen librarian, but I have had a good amount of frontline experience with kids. I also have the advantage of having traveled to almost every state and seen how libraries of all sizes in all different areas try to attract and serve teens.

First, remember that most kids are good kids, despite what the media may seem to suggest practically every day. Listen to the news long enough, and you would think that most of the young people who visit your branch are plotting to shoot up the school or are just thugs.

Library staff often lament that kids just "aren't raised right" anymore, as if the new generation must be clones of our personalities to be correct. The plain fact is that some library staff are afraid of kids simply because the kids they encounter often are so different than they themselves were when growing up.

Now, let's remember that everyone must abide by the rules of your library, and that includes the teens. Yes, I know we want them to come to the library. Yes, I know we want to be a "destination of choice" for these young people. Yes, I know we want to show them that we can give them the knowledge of the world and that it's all at their fingertips. But you cannot let them act any way they want just so you can have a full teen area and evidence of a high usage rate on your computers.

Some kids understand only the hard line, and if they do not comply with the library rules they can and should be ejected like anyone else. If you do not deny access to the kids who visit you for all the wrong reasons, then the students who honestly want to use the library for reading and studying will stop coming. Thus, you deny access to *them*.

The teen areas I have seen that are most successful are the ones that are adequately supervised. It is not a matter of not trusting the teens, but one of real-world necessity. If your teen center is a place where kids can be alone and do anything they want, you will more than likely have problems.

The frontline staff must be able to handle teens as well, and everyone must *like and enjoy* young people. How can you work in a library that is located right across the street from a school and not like kids? I see that situation often, and if you have the wrong team with the wrong mind-set, they will not be able to communicate with those kids. They must not be afraid of them, and they should get a sense of efficacy in helping them with their schoolwork.

I remember visiting a library where, I was told, a lot of kids "were just out of control." I entered the building right after school had let out, and there was indeed a sea of loud young patrons. It fascinated me that the staff members were all behind various desks or in the stacks, trying their best to ignore what was going on. It didn't take long for me to see that there was a "staff against teens" mentality. Thus, their progress was dead in the water.

We have to remember the tremendous social pressures that kids are subjected to these days. There is so much information available to them, especially with the Internet, and so many kids believe everything they read on the Web. Don't you remember how tough it was to discover your identity? Think of what a teen goes through now with exposure to so much information at such a young age.

We often forget how insecure some of us were and how we thought we had to cover up those feelings by posturing a certain way. Looking back, I know that many of the silly things I did as a kid resulted from not feeling quite good enough. Kids are kids, and I don't care if the fourteen-year-old kid is six feet tall; he is still fourteen and is thinking *like* a kid. Many of the library staff I know would do themselves a favor by giving the whole issue of teens a little thought rather than automatically dismissing and prejudging them when they come in the door.

Show your young patrons some respect and educate them to the purpose of the library. Give teens a little more leeway (but just a little) and an extra warning before you turn up the authority progressively if need be.

Many libraries I observe could help themselves with the afterschool student rush by simply limiting access to certain programs on certain computers during specific times. Before some of my librarian friends cringe and close the book, let me emphasize that I am not suggesting censorship, only managing your limited resources.

Let's say you have twenty computers in your library. The school bell rings and you become inundated with teens. They take over every available computer, and while some are doing schoolwork others are turning your computer area into a video arcade. And you have other groups hooting it up as they gather to look at Facebook or similar sites.

What is wrong with designating, during peak use times, only four of those computers for gaming? Another four could be used for Facebook and chatting. Then you keep the other twelve for research and schoolwork. This gives both students who are in the library for their homework and research products and *adults* who need to use a computer fair access to your limited computer resources.

If you have teen staff who can help control the use of the computers, then you probably don't have to consider this segmented approach (and I know some of my teen librarian friends are shuddering at this idea), but many smaller libraries do not have that type of staffing, so they may have to use other measures to control the environment. What if you don't have teen staff waiting for the kids to arrive so they can supervise all those activities?

Another matter to consider is making your teen area proportional to your overall square footage. Several times I have seen libraries trying to do too much with too little space, and it causes problems. A large teen area in a very small branch can overwhelm the rest of the library and your other patrons.

The layout of your building also makes a difference. If you have basically a large room divided into areas by the collection and not by walls, a loud, unsupervised teen area can disrupt other areas of the library. I have seen smaller libraries where the teens could be heard throughout the entire building.

And what about those moms and dads who let their younger children run through the building, climbing all over anything they can mount and making life hell for your other patrons? I usually handle this in one of two ways. Out of thousands of similar situations, I can remember only two or three instances where the parent balked at my saying anything.

If the kid is in imminent danger of getting hurt, I do approach him, but as easy as possible and in a way that shows nothing but my sincere concern for his safety. Let's say some tyke is climbing on that nice, abstract art sculpture that was donated to the library and sits by the circulation desk. Mom is busy checking out books and is oblivious to her child's plight (something I unfortunately see quite often). I ease up and say in a soft voice something like, "Whoa, hotshot. Careful. I'm afraid you might fall." I come on as low key as I can and avoid touching the child if at all possible. When Mom turns in response, I always smile and try to *make sure she does not think I am implying that she is a bad parent.* That is the main thing you do *not* want to convey. If you get the parent defensive, then she gets angry, and you have an unpleasant encounter. If I don't know where the parent is, I ask the kid where Mom or Dad is. If I don't get a response, I quickly get another staff member to come over so I am not alone with the child and then try to locate the parent.

If, in a different situation, a child is not about to immediately hurl to her doom but is well on her way, I locate the parent and say something like, "Excuse me, sir, is that your little one over there?" If you come up easy and smile, there is very, very rarely a problem. The parent sees what the tyke is doing and goes to get her. Usually I get a sincere thank-you, and I close by making a comment that I see such energetic kids get away from folks all the time because they are excited to be in the library. Get what I'm saying to them? Good kid, good parent.

Add these pointers to your procedures, and you will quickly see an improvement in patron compliance and employee confidence. You'll see how they blend in with the techniques in the next chapter.

Now ask yourself . . .

> Do you expect cooperation or confrontation with a patron who is breaking a rule?
>
> Are you being adequately cautious?
>
> What is your plan for patrons who will not cooperate?

5

PLAYING CHESS WITH THE CHECKERS PLAYER

Student: "People are strange, aren't they, master?"
Master: "Yes, we are."

—Traditional

My first security job was at a theme park on the border of North and South Carolina. I naturally wanted to do a good job, and I wanted to please my boss. I wanted patrons to comply, but I didn't want to make them angry. I didn't want to be disliked by them. I also wanted to be safe and certainly not have to engage in a physical confrontation. In other words, I wanted to do the best job I could and be an asset to the company and keep patrons safe. Does all this sound familiar?

When you entered the park, there were huge signs warning you that alcohol was not allowed anywhere on property. The signs turned out to be a poor deterrent (we all know that patrons rarely read signs). There was many a good ol' boy who wasn't about to pay what he considered high prices for food inside the park. He would bring his own refreshments and proceed to drop the tailgate and have a family picnic right in the parking lot.

Now here come me and my pals in a huge patrol car, an '80 Malibu. It was my job to approach and inform these folks that they could give me their beer, wine, liquor, or moonshine and stay, or they could keep it all and leave for the day. If they chose to keep the booze and leave, they did not get their admission fee back. I can remember one concert day in particular when I collected so much alcohol that twice I could not close the trunk of my patrol car. As you might imagine, I learned a lot about approaching people, and I learned it fast.

I was pretty successful and most folks, whether they liked it or not, complied, but I felt something was missing. Even though I was talking to several dozen patrons a day and hundreds on concert days, I didn't feel I had a good rhythm in my approach. I had created a few standard lines to apply, but really I was like a ship setting sail without a crew. I had no real strategy, and I was just not at the comfort level I wanted. I didn't understand the completely unpredictable reactions from patrons. There was no science to it. Then I remembered a lesson that was taught me many years earlier that had nothing to do with security work. It made all the difference in raising my confidence level in these situations.

WITH STRATEGY COMES CONFIDENCE

To help guide you along in this area, I have to share some personal history. Please stick with me as I explain how I developed my system for dealing with upset, irate, or just plain disturbed patrons. This concept is where the idea for *The Black Belt Librarian* originated.

During my early high school years, my grandfather overheard me talking about a bully who was torturing me on a daily basis. I was quite shy and had little self-esteem or confidence. My granddad knew of my interest in martial arts, so he bought me my first book on the subject, which gave me the impetus actually to join a karate class. That action would change my life in countless ways.

Karate schools back in the day were few and far between, and the ones that were around could be very intimidating. This one was certainly no different. At the tender age of fifteen, I was in my first Japanese Shotokan karate class, and I was in for much more than I had expected.

Those first years in karate were brutal. My instructor taught the way he was taught by his Japanese instructor, which meant seeing just how bad you *really* wanted to be in the class. It was a test of the spirit and will as much as it was how to throw a kick. We sparred with each other in class every night, and this was before all the foam rubber padding karate practitioners wear now. We were bare-fisted and -footed, and there were many teeth knocked out, collected, and placed back in. Protective headgear—what was that?

A classmate of mine broke another student's jaw in five places with a spinning kick. I once witnessed my instructor punch a fellow student smack in the nose one night just to see if he had the fortitude to come back to class. Our uniforms were speckled with blood, and it was impressed upon us that the red blotches were little badges of honor.

It was over the top by today's standards, but this was the Asian way to test your sincerity and character back in 1969. My instructor constantly pushed our willingness to stick things out, which was the price we paid to learn from him. It was damn scary at times and it did not come easy for me, but for some reason I did not quit. I was so very afraid. My staying must have just been fate. And I am telling you this, not to suggest how macho I am to have survived this, but to make the point that I really want to impress upon you.

Now there was plenty of technical information taught about how to execute all the various punches and kicks physically, but nothing to help me with the mental side of things. There was no psychological strategy for how to approach my sparring partner and, more important, no guidance on how to develop true confidence in myself—and that is why I had started practicing in the first place. My instructor would yell, "Get tough, Graham! You've got to be brave!" or "Hit with confidence! Don't be afraid! Go get 'em!" All this sounded good, but these were abstract terms. Either you had confidence and were naturally assertive or you weren't, and I wasn't. The more I thought about not being afraid, the more frightened I became.

I improved technically and eventually became a black belt, but I still really did not have true confidence in my abilities. *And how in the world can you optimally execute any type of action in your life if you don't honestly believe in yourself?*

I continued to experiment with different styles of martial art and eventually stumbled upon an instructor who helped me the most where I actually needed it—from the neck up, inside my head. How little did I know that what he taught me would one day apply directly to my day-to-day duties as a security officer?

My new instructor taught me how to approach different opponent types. Fighting, he said, was 90 percent mental. It wasn't as much about being physically tough as it was about developing skill in proper strategy. You don't just go in throwing punches, praying and hoping something connects, he pointed out. The informed martial artist alters his position according to the style of the fellow who is trying his best to knock his head off and out of the ring. Within days, this instructor had me feeling like I really knew what I was doing.

RECOGNIZING AND RESPONDING TO ANXIETY, BELLIGERENCE, OUT OF CONTROL, AND CALM

I could not control what my karate opponent was going to do, but by concentrating solely on my strategy I didn't have time for any type of fear or apprehension.

And the successful execution of my specific strategy, in turn, had a direct effect on limiting what my opponent could do against me, thus indirectly giving me the confidence I so needed. That approach worked then, I remembered, so could I adapt that idea to dealing with the public? Not in the physical way, of course, but in a mental capacity.

I started making notes about the patrons I encountered at the park. Who was upset and to what varying degrees? In karate I had four major types of opponents and developed strategies to handle what they would try to do to me. Gradually, through much examination and experimentation in the field, I came up with four levels of emotion to watch for in a patron and developed strategies for them as well.

By concentrating on a specific strategy that is best for the patron's current level of emotion, you also avoid the pressure of what my instructor said were "peripheral opponents." Let's say you are dealing with a patron who is upset about something and you are at the front desk. Often our minds start to go in all different directions. Instead of concentrating on the patrons, analyzing their emotional level and responding with a specific strategy, we start worrying about various things. Our fears surface and start to confuse us. What if I say the wrong thing? What do my coworkers think about what I'm saying? This patron looks pretty hostile. What if I can't handle this and she starts yelling at me? What will my boss think?

All of this has nothing to do with the task at hand. It is exactly like when I first started sparring. Instead of concentrating on my opponent, I was worried about what my girlfriend, family, or instructor would think if I lost. And what if I was kicked and hurt? What if I wasn't in shape and ran out of gas? What if my opponent was too tough for me? Fear can be a bottomless pit.

So you step up to the patron who wants to talk to you. It's a beautiful day (hey, maybe it's even payday) and you have just had a great lunch, but now you are faced with a first-rate, champion jerk. Here is what you must do:

1. Recognize that he is upset.
2. Ascertain the emotional level at which he is operating.
3. Respond with the strategy for that specific emotional state.
4. Concentrate and center on effecting your plan.

I use the acronym ABCC to remember these four emotional states, one of which anyone is experiencing at any given time. It stands for anxiety; belligerence; (out of) control; and calm. I put them in this alphabetical order because it's easy to remember, but these levels do not necessarily run in any order, so keep that in mind. I could try to impress you with fancier terms or a longer list, but there is no need; that's not my style and I am here to help you in the real world. This is what I use daily and it works for me. The simpler it is, the easier it is to retain under stress. Let's examine them one by one.

ANXIETY

You occasionally have patrons who are upset about something, real or imagined. They are in a state of *anxiety* and agitated to some mild degree. There can be any number of reasons why a patron anxious. The most common is the stress the average person is under today—time, money, commitments, all on a higher level than ever before—and it can wear anyone out. And we are living in an age of instant access, so folks tend to want what they are after *right bloody now*. Just think of how computer speed has changed in the past five years and how you can get irritated because your computer may be slow on a given day, even though it provides the knowledge of the world at your fingertips.

We are also overstimulated. With so many news sources assaulting our senses with continuous, mostly negative news via our computers, newspapers, and televisions, it is no wonder many patrons can be on the edge.

Sometimes they come in defensive to start with. They have had a previous negative experience with the library or somewhere else, so they step up to the desk a little edgy.

You can certainly be a victim of their bias before you even say anything to them. They don't like you because of your gender, race, profession, or Lord only knows what else. They don't give you a chance, and you haven't even opened your mouth yet.

Occasionally you are the victim of what I call the "first *no* phenomenon"—when the patron doesn't believe you when you tell him he can't do what he wants to do. He asks to speak to someone else to see if that person also will tell him something can't be done, just to make sure you know what you're talking about.

Sometimes they just don't understand what you are trying to tell them, and they get frustrated and vent that toward you. Keep in mind that those D and F students we went to school with are still out there roaming the hills, and libraries, somewhere.

You will also have patrons who just don't know how to express themselves in any way but mean or nasty. My boss Nina Lyon and I used to have a laugh when she would remind me that "some people just aren't raised right." My grandmother would nudge me and observe that "some people are just mean as hell." You know, they were both right, and that sums up some of the patrons I deal with as well as anything else I have heard or read.

The most important thing you can do when you recognize someone in a state of anxiety is to stop what you are doing, look into her eyes, and actively listen. That's what I said: stop, look, and listen.

This is simple advice, but sometimes very hard to do when chaos reigns on your job. You have a line out the door, you are one employee short, so you can't take your lunch and your blood sugar is dropping. You are running out of change and now you can't find that book on hold that a patron has driven thirty miles for. Nevertheless, once you sense a state of anxiety in a patron, that is what you must do. Stop what you are doing. Look at her. Listen to what she tells you. If you give her your undivided attention for just a couple of minutes, that's usually all it takes to get her back to the calm level where you want her. Even if she doesn't get what she wants, at least she will probably be satisfied that someone honestly listened to her. And isn't that what everyone wants when they are upset?

The last thing you want to do is mimic the level of emotion an anxious patron is in, which I saw happen once when a staff member reacted to a frustrated patron by saying, "Well, if you think you have problems, just come around the desk and work with me for an hour!" No need to tell you what the patron did after she heard that.

Watch your body language and countenance; no crossed arms, hands on hips, or frowning. Soften your speech and go a little lower than the patron's, and he will focus in on what you are saying more. And never forget the solid gold tactic of introducing yourself, getting the patron's name, and using it often during the conversation.

So hear these patrons out and let them vent a little. We all get upset sometimes. Demonstrate a little honest empathy, and that will usually neutralize any anger. And if the library was wrong (yes, sometimes the patron *is* right and knows what he is talking about), apologize, promise to follow up, and make sure you do so.

To give you an idea of the mood and pace you are attempting to set, here are some phrases you can use:

> "We're here to help you, and we're going to get this all worked out." You are trying to make them feel at ease that you are interested in what they have to say.

> "I understand what you're saying." This is positive reinforcement that they are indeed being heard.

"If I don't have an answer for you, I'll find it." Again, you are sending the message of how intent you are to help them as much as you can. And even though I say this, I rarely have to call in help, since the patrons are usually satisfied I have sincerely done everything I can for them.

"I need to ask some questions to make it easier for us to correct this." At this point I pull out my ever-present notepad or grab a piece of scratch paper. This also lets them know you are listening and want to assist.

Mishandling patrons during this stage of emotion is what most often gets you complained about. Please remember that your recognition of their anxiety and your control of it by applying the proper strategy can keep things from getting much worse.

BELLIGERENCE

At this stage a patron may begin really raising his voice or yelling. He may be cursing the library or the circumstances, but not *you* specifically. Other patrons can't help but hear, and some may be startled. This is when you *must* take a stand and establish your credibility with the patron immediately, before things get worse. This is critical and must be done quickly if you hope to gain control of the situation.

Here are a few ideas for what you could say:

"I'm ready to discuss this with you as long as it takes; I'm here to help you. But I'm not going to let you yell at me."

"This is not helping us resolve things. Please settle down and we'll get it worked out." Never tell anyone to "calm down." That is too clichéd and doesn't work well.

"I need you to please lower your voice; I want to help you."

"You've asked me, so please let me explain this to you."

This is the worst time to lose your own temper, but I have seen it happen many times. "I'll have your job." "Oh yeah? Well, I get off work at five and I'll twist your head like a doorknob!" Don't be emotional. Don't feel like you have to prove yourself or one-up the patron. Leave your ego out of things. These patrons do not actually know you, so don't take their comments or actions personally.

Another important point is to keep eye contact with the patron as you talk to him. Does that prospect make you nervous? Use a little game of looking at his eyebrows or looking at one eye and then the other. This, for some reason I can't explain, alleviates some of the pressure you may feel when you need to stay face-to-face.

Learning to stand your ground with a patron can be more than a little intimidating at first, but the absolute worst thing you can do is to shrink away and let the patron rant on. He then often gets even more caught up in his own emotions. Once you communicate that his behavior is not going to be allowed, the patron usually settles back to at least the anxiety stage.

OUT OF CONTROL

The third stage to discuss is one I hope you never see, but you probably will if you work with the public long enough. The patron has lost control and is cursing you specifically. She may be throwing things or damaging property. She may be communicating threats to you. She may even be drunk or high. This is the *out-of-control* stage of emotion. Now is the time to call your security or the police. The patron has checked out of Hotel Reality, and it is time to take immediate measures to protect yourself. Do not hesitate to call for help when things have deteriorated to this point.

You may be asking yourself if I expect you to pick up the phone and call for help in the face of someone threatening you. Yes, I do. I have found that if the patron is going to assault you, she has already made up her mind, somewhere deep down, to do so. You are far better off attempting to call for assistance. Even if you only get a chance to push 911 before she actually physically attacks you, help will be on its way.

Another reason this action is the smart play is that I have seen calling for help as a way of establishing your credibility with the patron. I have witnessed some extremely irate people come around quickly when they saw that the police were being called despite their best bullying display of emotion. You may also choose to take this action when they are in the belligerence stage if you think that, despite your best efforts, the out-of-control stage is imminent.

I am not guaranteeing anyone's safety by telling you to call for help. I can't tell you what a patron may always do in reaction. But I do know that when you are threatened or feel unsafe, any police officer would tell you to call. When things get to this level, this is not child's play. This is as serious as it gets, so call 911. You are better off doing this than just standing there.

So now you have just handled a particularly challenging situation with a behavior problem and find yourself shaking like a leaf. What is going on? you ask. I was right, he was definitely wrong. Why is this upsetting me so much?

You have probably heard of the fight-or-flight reaction. The idea is that long ago our primitive ancestors with their tiny, undeveloped brains could react only one of two ways in the face of real danger. Og, the caveman, goes over the hill and meets up with a very hungry saber-toothed tiger. His reaction-based brain signals either to take off running back across the hill or to stand and fight. That limbic system is still part of our brains today; it is sometimes referred to as our "emotional brain," among other things. It has no sense of time or logic, and it has not evolved. Even though we have frontal lobes that Og didn't, they haven't quite caught up with overruling our emotions. You could say it is still prehistoric. It is there to sense danger and make us react in time to save ourselves.

So what happens when this kicks in? Immediately your energy goes to your larger muscles to enable you to run faster or fight harder. Your fine-motor skills go out the window. Thus, your hands shake and your knees quiver. Your adrenaline dumps and you become warm and flushed. You may get butterflies in your stomach.

Understand that you are *not* falling apart. It is not raw fear you are experiencing. All this is nature's way of gearing you up for a confrontation, and nothing more. If you didn't feel these things to some extent, it wouldn't be natural.

Remember to breathe deeply, for your shortened breath denies oxygen to your brain, thus hampering your thinking. Understand these feelings for what they are, and you will be able to deal with them better than you ever thought you could.

When I had to call the police, that meant that the patron was going to leave the library for the maximum amount of time—and that meant permanently.

CALM

The level of emotion you see most often is *calm*. Your patrons come in to get their materials, you have a pleasant interaction, and all is good with the world. At times, however, patrons may start off calm until you tell them about the $40 they owe in lost-book charges. They may go into any of the other stages quickly.

Be wary of a patron who has been out of control and then becomes calm. Be careful, because he can flip back to out-of-control behavior like the flicking of a light switch. I witnessed a fellow throw a chair through a plate glass window, then fall to his knees sobbing like a baby, apologizing and trying to write a check for the damage. The police had been notified and were on the way, but five minutes later and before they could get there he was trying to throw another chair.

BANNING PATRONS AND KEEPING THEM OUT

I do believe that some patrons should never receive a second chance. Along with the examples mentioned earlier, this should include patrons who expose themselves, grope a patron, and similar actions. I once knew a librarian who loved to say, "Everyone deserves a second chance, Warren." But do you think someone masturbating at a computer in broad daylight deserves that consideration from you? Do you think banning him for the month is going to change his behavior?

Remember that patrons *get themselves* banned. What are you to do, after all? A patron does not comply with the rules of the library despite your best efforts. Does she get a pass because nothing you say or do works with her?

Who on earth comes to the library drunk or whacked out on drugs? Who would think that a library is a place to go and wash both clothes and self (and throw in a shave, too)? Who comes to a library to stalk women or try to touch them or just glare at them all day?

And how does one get banned from a library, anyway? It always amazed me that people could not or would not control themselves in a library setting, especially when they later told me they had nowhere else to go. Many said that they were even banned from the local homeless facilities, which brings up another question: if shelters ban their patrons for not adhering to their rules, and schools and community centers suspend kids for disallowed behavior, why would any library think they have to put up with the same disruptive behavior?

So, you have someone who will not go along with the simple, reasonable rules of the library and refuses to leave when asked. That is another example of out-of-control behavior, and that person should be ejected and banned.

It is truly fascinating to me that so many libraries have such extensive policies regarding zero tolerance for internal workplace problems, yet many excuse patrons, no matter how belligerent or aggressive they are to staff members.

So THERE YOU have it. My strategies for any of the four levels of emotion your patron/"opponent" may go through. They are all field-tested, and I used them every day. As you practice and get your rhythm, you will see firsthand that this approach has an extremely high success rate. No strategy works all the time, but these will serve you well in the majority of situations—I would say 95 percent or better.

But now we have to take a step back yet again to look at the toughest person you will really ever have to deal with. Do you remember? We touched on this individual in chapter 3. The biggest adversary you will ever come up against is yourself. How will you handle your emotions? How will you recognize what is happening to you before it sabotages you? How do you stay in control? What do you say to the person in the mirror?

A good friend of mine at work would often ask me the same question regarding my handling of problem patrons. Invariably, he and I would be walking around and discussing some library matter, when I would see a behavior problem and stop to correct it without incident. My friend was always amazed. "How do you do that?" he asked. "How can you just suddenly shift gears like that and then actually get them to listen to you?" It was a great compliment, but as I have admitted to you, it was never easy or natural for me; I simply developed a procedure that helped me become good at it. Again, I remind you to work on it diligently and that it takes time.

The best way to keep your head in a tense situation is to simply know what you are doing and to have confidence in both your and the library's strategy for dealing with security situations. You may not naturally have self-confidence, or you may have the tendency to doubt yourself in these situations, but the next best thing is to have confidence in your strategies. You must have a plan of action that you can apply regardless of how you feel physically or emotionally at any give time. That is what made the critical difference for me.

Self-efficacy is a simple formula. It is the natural outcome of consistently applying correct, basic fundamentals and nothing more. It is not complicated, but you do need to learn to focus and stabilize your mind by concentrating on your plan. That is how you keep your cool.

Now ask yourself . . .

> Do you know the different types of patrons' emotional levels?
>
> Does your library make it perfectly clear when you should call the police?
>
> Do you know what kinds of behavior must lead to banning and how long the ban should be?

6

DAY-TO-DAY SECURITY CONSIDERATIONS

In today's world, true innovation means getting back to the basics.

—Albert Einstein

As I TRAVEL around the country visiting libraries, I see the same problems over and over again. In this chapter I offer some basic (and necessary, in my opinion) procedures for you to always be aware of that can make all the difference in keeping you and your coworkers safe. These are things you can do every day. I also review some security-related elements of library design. Some of this information is essentially useful only during design planning, but there are often ways you can improve even an unfortunate design.

WHAT YOU CAN DO IMMEDIATELY TO MAKE THE LIBRARY SAFER

1. Never, and I mean never, count money in view of patrons. Make up your deposits and balance the register or cash drawer before you open or after you close. Gone is the day you can run your library like Sam Drucker's general store in Hooterville (I'm really dating myself with that one). I've seen staff hurry in at *five minutes* before opening. They cut on the lights and maybe do a personal thing or two and open the doors to the public. Then they get out the cash and make sure it is counted properly, right in front of patrons. It looks like they are running some wheel-of-fortune game in Vegas. But that's okay, right? Because, after all, you've "never had a problem before" (remember chapter 2).

You open with, say, only $50, so you think that doesn't offer a robber enough. Well, the robber doesn't know how much you have. All a thief sees is the green you are handling. People are hurt for much less, and $50 is a lot of money to a destitute person.

2. Whether you have money drawers or cash registers, make sure they stay locked when you are away from the circulation desk. Countless libraries are ripped off because there is no one at the desk and the drawer is not locked. If you are working up front and it's busy, it is acceptable to have it unlocked, but *at any other time,* lock up. And please, locking the drawer and leaving the key in the lock is not really securing it, is it?

Circulation staff can have a key to the drawer that they carry with them. Don't have a key at the front desk on a huge dowel marked CASH DRAWER or REGISTER. I would laugh along with you, but I have actually seen that one so much it's depressing.

3. Keep library keys with you at all times, and don't leave them lying around. Put them on one of those little coil gizmos that fits around your wrist or on a lanyard. Belt clips work too. If you have so many keys that they weigh you down, it is way past the time to rekey the building.

4. Be very careful in handling your deposits. There is no such thing as a night deposit. Always take money to the bank during regular business hours. Break up the times you go as best you can. Don't always go, for example, every Tuesday and Thursday at high noon.

I will never forget what I saw during a visit to the Midwest, when arriving at a library with my host. We saw the branch manager going across the lot with a bank bag with the bank's name clearly marked on the side. He waved at us with the bag and shouted from across the lot, "I didn't know you guys would be here so soon. I always go to the bank about one o'clock."

5. Never leave your pocketbook or briefcase where it can be seen by patrons. I know this can be inconvenient at times, but if you are ever ripped off it makes for a dangerous environment because the thief now thinks your library is an easy mark, and he *will* return. And if you, a fellow employee, or a patron catch him in the act, he could assault someone. Always secure these items.

6. Staff areas should be locked at all times. Staff areas should be locked at all times. Staff areas should be locked at all times. No, this is not a misprint. Staff areas should be locked at all times. You never want to walk into back rooms or offices and find someone who is not supposed to be there.

7. Double-check all bathrooms, stacks, study rooms, and the rest of the public areas to make sure all patrons are out before you close. You do not want to be alone with some unknown individual after closing. If you think you might have trouble with someone at closing, call the police well before you start closing procedures so you won't be by yourself with the potential problem.

8. Never let anyone other than authorized library staff or service contractors into the building before opening or after closing. If you have not been advised that Billy Bob's Carpet Cleaning is coming, don't let them in. The same goes for the telephone guy here to "check the phone lines." He had better have some ID, and you had better ask him for it.

9. Working alone in the library building is one of the most dangerous things you can do. Take a look at scheduling to see if there is anything you can do to avoid being there by yourself. Maybe you can get a part-time page or ask for a volunteer to be there with you. When alone, keep your phone use and duties to an absolute minimum. The standard rule is *the less staff on hand, the more your awareness goes up*. I know this is difficult, because you still have a library to operate, but pay as much attention to who is in the building and what they are doing as you possibly can.

Never admit to being alone to a patron you don't really know. If a patron asks you if you are by yourself, say something like, "No, Jeff is in the back, but he's also busy. One of us will be with you in a moment." Although such an inquiry is usually innocent, there is no point in exposing your vulnerability.

These points are the main short-term things you need to consider. I would bet that you recognize something in this list that you can change. Let me just warn you that old habits die hard, and some employees are often negative about changing their ways, even if it is for their own safety. And of the staff members who are already safety minded, there are even fewer who will readily go along with new procedures if they are seemingly inconvenient to them. But as the saying goes, "The only thing that doesn't change is change," so it is part of staff members' jobs to adapt and help make the workplace safer for everyone.

DESIGNING A SECURE LIBRARY

I see the same basic, intrinsic design problems in many libraries. You must watch the process of planning a building carefully, for you do not want to be in the position of having to "fight" it daily. I am sure many of you have learned this lesson the hard way. Your building should enhance and add to security rather than detract from it by creating even more problems for the staff.

Here are the design problems I encounter most often, in no particular order. Please avoid them in the first place or try to correct them if you are already stuck with them:

circulation desks too far from the entrance or book alarm

teen areas that cannot be seen by staff or are not staffed

computer areas set up where you cannot readily see screens

no doors on staff areas

bathrooms in vestibule areas where staff cannot see them

children's areas that have gone overboard with a "playland" environment

Circulation desks that are too far from the book alarm or entrance make it difficult for staff to address a possible theft situation when the alarm sounds. You don't want to have to yell across the room to question someone, which can be awkward for you as well as a patron. You can easily embarrass someone into a verbal or even physical situation by appearing to come on too strong. And if the patron does not respond to your long-distance inquiry, it is usually impossible to get over to her quickly, and then she is out the door and long gone.

I cover the problem of teen areas more thoroughly in chapter 4, but it bears repeating. Every time I have seen a teen area that is not supervised or cannot be seen clearly by staff, it results in problems. Put it where you can see it. It is not about trust, it is about a bunch of kids, period. Yes, I know this answer will upset some of the teen librarians I know, but I am asked about this constantly in my travels, and simply making the young adult area more visible often immediately makes things more controllable.

If you are going to limit what patrons can view in your computer area, you should place the computer screens facing a staff desk, so the patrons' backs are to the staff. This is a huge deterrent. If you were coming to the library to look at things that you were not supposed to, you would go where no one could easily see the screen. Have filters? Well, they help, but if you think they are stopping everyone from accessing porn sites, you are very mistaken. The same goes for those recessed screens and privacy screens. Those are the computers such users go to first.

And, yes, I know that some libraries allow patrons to look at anything they want, but from my experience those libraries generally have more problems than the libraries that have limitations for patrons.

Again, your staff areas need to be locked, and you have to have doors in the first place. So many libraries just have big openings in the wall that lead to employee areas, and they make me cringe. I have heard so many stories over the years about bad people in restricted areas, so if you do have doors, please, please secure them. Certainly this is a pain, since you go through some of these doors a hundred times a day. That's just too bad. Please learn from the countless libraries I have visited that have had problems occasioned by unsecured staff rooms. Staff areas need doors, and they need to be locked.

A common design in newer libraries is a big vestibule area that includes a meeting room and bathrooms. This is nice and convenient for patrons and usually a nightmare for staff. The staff can't see the restrooms, and after an incident they can't tell who did what or when.

I often visit children's rooms where the staff are crying the blues about parents bringing their kids in and letting them go wild. What they don't realize is that they have often created a playland, in an effort to be kid friendly, that encourages such behavior. Honestly, if I had not worked in a library and taken my two-year-old to some of these areas, I would naturally think that the library wanted my kid to run and play. So you have to watch this. I have seen buildings with unique areas that are quite beautiful and certainly get the child's attention without giving them twenty ways to fall to their doom.

And let me say a word or two about having video cameras, since I am always asked about this. I have changed my opinion on this recently, having traveled and seen so many different types of library designs. I am now of the opinion that, yes, most libraries (not all, but most) need some type of a camera system, a basic one at the very least. What I mean by *basic* is camera locations that are recording patrons both entering and leaving the library, showing them at the angles and with the clarity to identify them if needed. This way, if you ban someone, you do not have to worry about getting a picture. With good, well-placed cameras and a digital recorder, it is a simple matter to review the recorded data and print a photo from the monitor screen.

This setup is also vitally important if a child is ever taken from the library, so all managers need to know how to work the camera and recording equipment properly and expediently.

Some libraries need more extensive camera positioning. Fortunately, with technology advancing the way it always is, the cost of these systems is coming down all the time. Be sure to get two or three vendors' bids, but don't sacrifice quality for the low bid. You get what you pay for.

And while we are talking about cameras, forget about dummy camera locations. It does not cost that much more to get the real thing, and you do not want to promote a false sense of security.

Are cameras an invasion of privacy, as a seminar attendee recently asked me? No. You are not sitting around a panel of monitors zooming in to see what a patron is reading. Your cameras are there for everyone's safety. You are also showing that you are attempting to be good stewards of the public's property—the facility, books, and other materials—by using cameras to help prevent mutilation or theft. Most patrons, times being what they are, expect to see reasonable security measures in place.

Now ask yourself . . .

What are your current vulnerabilities as a library?

Do you change procedures proactively when you see that a change is needed?

What can you change about your building's layout to make it safer?

7

A STRATEGY FOR BASIC SECURITY DOCUMENTATION

The great artist is the simplifier.

—Henri-Frédéric Amiel

PROPER DOCUMENTATION—SO VITAL, yet often so underused in the security area of operating a library. The library administration needs it to justify monies spent on adequate staffing, mirrors, cameras, security staff, and the like. Ongoing, monthly, and yearly tracking shows trends in various problem areas. Staff use it to communicate effectively to the administration what is needed on the front line to provide a secure environment for patrons as well as themselves.

I have seen all kinds of security report forms in my career. For some reason, a lot of people think that the more complicated they are, the more effective they are. What lengthy forms usually do is raise your sense of anxiety over being involved in an incident, and thus having to be a part of the report process. Some forms are so complicated that staff do anything to avoid them, and that includes ignoring situations that need to be documented.

In this chapter I offer several forms to help you that are quite simple and multifunctional. They are not the only forms you may eventually need, but they are a vital start. And if you are in a smaller library they may indeed serve all your purposes.

DAILY SECURITY LOG

At the beginning of each day, you start off with a new security log (figure 7.1). At the top you see several headings. "Type" is to be filled in with either an asterisk or one of the other incident type codes listed at the bottom of the log. The # column is used for assigning the incident a number. "Time" is simply the time whatever you are notating took place. The "Staff" and "Police/Medic" columns list those who first noticed or responded to the situation. Other staff involved are added in the "Narrative" column.

Suppose a group of teenagers have food and beverages in the library business section. You tell them that food is not allowed, and they comply by taking it all outside to finish. On your log you put an asterisk under "Type" to denote a *rule advisement,* the time you advised them, and your name, and then you just write in

SECURITY LOG

Day: _____ Date: _____

TYPE	#	TIME	STAFF	POLICE/ MEDIC	NARRATIVE
AD	11-0001	10 am	Smith	Sgt. Lee	John Doe permanently banned for intoxication.

Type codes: A=Assault; AD=Alcohol/Drugs; BT=Bomb Threat; CM=Computer Misuse; DC=Disorderly Conduct; DTP=Damage to Property; FA=Fire Alarm; EI=Employee Injury; MRI=Miscellaneous Rule Infraction; PI=Patron Injury; SOL=Soliciting; TH=Theft; TR=Trespass; O=Other; *=Rule Advisement

FIGURE 7.1

what happened in the right-hand column, for example, "Advised four patrons they could not eat in the library."

Now imagine instead that this group gives you a hard time and refuses to dispose of their food. You make your best effort to communicate with them, but nothing works. So you decide that they have to leave for the day and eject them. This would now be a *security incident,* not just a rule advisement. On the log you list MR under "Type" for *miscellaneous rule infraction.* You write in the time and your name or that of the staff member who ejected them. The "Narrative" might go something like "Group of patrons, previously advised no food allowed at (note time of original warning), refused to comply. I warned them that if they did not dispose of the food, they would have to leave for the day. They chose to leave."

If you know the names of the group members, they could be added to your report. The whole incident narrative is written on the log, taking up as many lines as necessary. As you record all incidents during the day, you are combining notations for every time you advise someone of rule infractions (which helps document for the administration how busy you are with controlling the library environment) with more involved security incidents.

Assigning the incident number in the # column is simple. On your computer, make a log of your incidents as they occur. Give each one a six-digit number. Make the first two digits the year, such as 11-0001. The next incident will be 11-0002, and so forth.

Now imagine another incident. A man is obviously very intoxicated and trying to ask everyone for money. You call your security or the police. When they arrive, they obtain his name and inform him of his ban. On your security log you enter AD under "Type" for *alcohol/drugs.* Then list the time and initial staff and responding officer and write up the who, what, when, and where in the "Narrative" column, again using as many lines as you need.

Your security log may become a court document, so print or write neatly and use only black ink. Keep the narrative brief and professional. I prefer a handwritten log so I can move around with it on a clipboard if necessary, but you could put this on a computer and use it that way.

If the police or a medic ever has to be called, note their names in the column provided. When a *situation* officially becomes an *incident* is up to you, but once you call the police or medic to help, it is an incident.

Figure 7.1 is just a sample form, and when you create your own, you can of course revise it as you think appropriate. Store paper forms or save them in a computer for posterity. I still have my first library security report from June 1989. You never know when you may need them for some type of court proceeding.

TRESPASS LOG

For easy reference, make another list of the names of people you ban as well as the date and length of the ban (figure 7.2). If you don't have a name, you can enter some nickname to know them by, but as in the potential problem log (see below), make sure the moniker does not show bias. You can modify my version of this form anyway you need to, but you get the idea. You have a sheet for every letter of the alphabet and enter names last name first.

Notice that in the right-hand column you can enter a police report number, if applicable. You could also add another column for the length of the ban if your library has several different ban periods.

Cross-reference this form with your incident number so you can easily go back to the respective daily security log for details of the incident. Now you can look up the banned patrons by name instead of first going through all the incident logs.

POTENTIAL PROBLEM LOG

Now take a look at the potential problem log (figure 7.3). This is a simple way of tracking patrons who are acting suspiciously. Or maybe you have corrected someone's behavior and your heightened awareness (which you are already working to develop) tells you that this patron is probably someone you will have to deal with again.

You see a place for the person's name and description as well as room for several incidents. For any incident, just write in a narrative of what you observed. This is for future reference, in case you ever need to talk to or eject this person again. The record gives you more justification for whatever action you might have to take.

Describe the offender as best you can and note the name if you have it. I usually didn't have a name, so I had to come up with some type of moniker. But when you do this, remember to keep it professional and not prejudicial or demeaning. There is a big difference between referring to an unknown behavior problem as "Magazine Man" and as "Dirty Old Bastard #2." The latter implies a bias you don't want to have to defend if your log turns out to be needed as a court document.

TRESPASS LOG

LAST NAME BEGINS WITH D _____

NAME	RACE	SEX	DATE OF WARNING	SECURITY OFFICER	POLICE OFFICER	INCIDENT NUMBER	PICTURE	PROBLEM	POLICE REPORT NUMBER
Doe, John	W	M	4.29.11	Smith	Lee	11-0001	Yes	Intox	7382

FIGURE 7.2

POTENTIAL PROBLEM LOG

Subject's Name: _____

Description: _____

_____

_____

Date: _____ Entered by: _____

Problem: _____

_____

Date: _____ Entered by: _____

Problem: _____

_____

Date: _____ Entered by: _____

Problem: _____

_____

Date: _____ Entered by: _____

Problem: _____

_____

FIGURE 7.3

Some people are hard to describe, so the work (I really wouldn't refer to this as "work"; it's really just life in a public institution these days) is in you communicating to your coworkers when you write someone up. If the person is still in the library, discreetly show him to as many staff as you can. Next time you see him, pass the information on to staff who were not present at the incident. This is just basic communication in a safe workplace. And why wouldn't you do this? You can't control who comes through the door, so don't you want to control everything internally that you possibly can?

Let me emphasize that by utilizing this procedure, you are not profiling people or setting them up to be banned or "putting them under a microscope." You are just being smart. If your intuition tells you that there is the possibility of future problems with the patron, there is no harm in noting this on such a log and passing the information along to your coworkers. Many patrons I entered in such logs over the years I never saw again, and many returned and were never any problem. But I always continued to heed that little voice that told me to pay attention, and you should too.

Now, INSTEAD OF just telling the boss how busy you are with security, you can show her with three cumulative totals every month: total reported incidents, total times you have corrected behavior, and total potential problems.

Keep up with these on a simple recap sheet with a spreadsheet program. This will show what is really happening on the front line. The more divorced your administration is from dealing with the public, the more you need this documentation.

Now ask yourself . . .

How effective is your current documentation?

Can you justify your security budget?

Do you analyze trends in your building and your branches?

8

SECURITY PERSONNEL WHO ACTUALLY HELP YOU BE SECURE

Is there anyone so wise as to learn from the past?

—Voltaire

Aн, тне issue of security personnel. I am asked about this constantly in my travels. Let me just cover what I know should be your concerns with hiring security staff.

WHAT TO LOOK FOR IN A SECURITY OFFICER

You must have the right people carrying badges around your building and talking with your patrons, and I may be the first to tell you that they are not easy to find. They have to like people (patrons *and* staff) and get a sense of efficacy when they help them. They should never think of anyone asking them for assistance as a nuisance or bother.

They must be well groomed and always on task. You want professional, well-trained, and objective individuals who readily give the public the benefit of the doubt and resolve incidents in the library's best interest.

Also, your officers need to move around on a timely basis. This means no hanging out behind the reference or other public service desk or engaging in prolonged conversations with other staff.

They have to be mature. You cannot have some John Wayne strutting around with his spurs jingling and jangling thinking that he must "out-tough" everyone to get them to comply. That type of security will get you into trouble very quickly. Your security staff must be confident and secure with themselves.

Officers have to know how to get past the "barrier of the badge," as I like to call it. Many people who resent authority may come into your library, and when they see your officer they are going to have a chip on their shoulder. It takes a talent to be able to stay relaxed and flow with a situation that involves a behavior problem who throws everything your officer says back in his face.

Officers must be able to communicate a negative in the most positive way possible. I cannot emphasize this point enough. You cannot train security staff to have a sincere interest in and empathy with patrons; they must bring that to the job.

Security people have to stay off their butts most of the time and be both visible and vigilant. I can put anyone in a chair with a coffee and newspaper, but I want an "officer," and not a "guard." I want the officer moving around and observing possible behavior problems before they see the officer. I want security staff who innately understand this core principle. Someone who wants to sit at a desk with her head buried in a crossword puzzle will never understand this.

I think that officers should be in reasonable physical shape. This has always been a tick of mine as a security manager. Mind you, I don't mean looking like the cover of a fitness magazine; I just want my staff to able to move quickly and adequately come to your aid without being hindered by a lack of fitness. Can they go up the steps to help you, or do they need to wait on the elevator? This qualification also goes along with my opinion that officers should be standing and moving around most of the time and not sitting, which requires reasonable fitness.

And what if the officers have to defend themselves or others? You need to arrange for proper training of defensive techniques. You can theorize that your library does not want the officers to have to touch someone, but if you are in a problematic library, sooner or later they will have to. That is just the way it is. Some behavior problems only understand the hard line, and you do not want officers to be too vulnerable. Keep in mind also that you will document the training of security techniques, so if an officer ever goes further than necessary you have proof of how she was trained. This will help if you ever face litigation.

A security officer must be someone you can trust to do the job, being visible and vigilant even when the manager isn't around. A strong work ethic and sense of responsibility are absolutely critical. I always told my security staff that the library could not function properly without us, and I meant that.

Make sure your security staff can express themselves in written form as well as verbally. Reports can become court documents and need to be written in a

professional manner. During the interview process, have them write out a description of the most difficult incident they have ever handled and see for yourself how
they do. This is an important skill that they must have. There is a big difference
between "Let's eat Grandma" and "Let's eat, Grandma."

As it is with the rest of the library staff, consistency is critical when it comes to
security matters. Security officers must function as a unit and all follow the same
procedures day in and day out. An officer who is more stringent with banning, or
notably less so, than the other security staff could be accused of some type of bias.

THE LOOK OF A PROFESSIONAL

When it comes to dressing the security staff, and I again stress simplicity. I always
clothed my staff with plain black slacks and blue polo shirts with the library logo
on the front and SECURITY added. I also provided jackets and caps with the same
logo. They wore a North Carolina Security Officer badge in a clip holder on the
right front of their belt. They carried handcuffs only; no pepper spray or baton or
any other weapon. I wanted their weapons to be their minds. I wanted them to use
their wits rather than automatically fall back on some physical weapon. This was
in our particular security environment. There may be environments or contexts
where traditional weapons are justified, such as in a multiple building setting or
late-night patrols, but we were not in that position.

I had worked in positions where I wore a more classic guard uniform. I found
that most experienced behavior problems thought I was the typical guard from a
contract service, so they assumed I was ill trained and unsure and often tried to
take advantage of that assumption. I did not want my staff to be underestimated in
any way, so I uniformed them much differently. Indeed, I have seen uniforms taken
to their logical absurdity, with a myriad of patches, whistles, broad-rimmed hats
with badges atop, and the like—so much so that they looked like the Village People.

I have also seen formal, classic-style uniforms that could work, ones that are
extremely close to police uniforms with custom patches (rather than the generic
SECURITY OFFICER patch you can get on the Internet) and badges. Even then, it is
best to keep the accessories to a minimum. The uniforms also need to fit the officer.
Nothing looks worse than a uniform just off the rack and two sizes too big.

I learned by utilizing different uniforms that subtle, or "soft," is better. Although
there are exceptions, generally I prefer polo shirts as previously described. I wore
athletic shoes and certainly allowed my staff to do the same, but they had to be solid

black ones—no color stripes or insignias. I supplied the uniforms, but it was up to the officers to keep them cleaned and pressed.

CONTRACT OR PROPRIETARY OFFICERS?

In regards to utilizing contract companies or hiring your own in-house staff, I strongly recommend a proprietary approach. It has been my experience that contractual security firms rarely work out. Am I saying that none of those guards know what they are doing? No, of course not; I hired my assistant in Charlotte when all he had was contract company experience. But from all that I have seen and heard, dealing with the various consequences of going the contract route is, more often than not, problematic at best.

Even at the library in Charlotte, the county periodically raised the subject of contract security in an effort to cut every penny that they possibly could. This always amazed me, since the repeated and total failure of several contract security companies is what directly led to my being hired and initiating a proprietary security staff.

Hiring your own security staff can be difficult enough. Good help is hard to find, as the old saying goes, and that is even truer when it comes to security personnel. But that doesn't mean you can't find it. If they are your own staff, you have infinitely more control over them. With your own staff, you know exactly how they are trained. You know about their backgrounds and personalities because you interview them, perform record checks, and hire them. You have immediate authority to correct any shortcomings, to write them up, or even to terminate them.

Your own staff usually also care much more about the facility than a contracted employee. To many contract staff, your library is just another gig, and it is rare to find someone who will go the extra mile and step up in difficult situations like your own hire would. They know that if you don't like them, their company will just assign them elsewhere with little or no consequence.

If your budget allows you to hire contract officers only, remember never to hesitate to demand a replacement, period. You are paying for a service, and if an officer does not meet your requirements the company must respond to your concern quickly. The officer is there to prevent and solve problems, not to be one. Do not allow a poor return on your investment. Monitor security staff when they work for you, and make sure they are doing what you need them to do. Do not assume that they have the same feeling of responsibility for your library that you do.

The security company you contract needs to know from the start that you will execute this plan when you are not satisfied with performance. Give the company a list of expectations for their employees so they know what to expect when they work for you. Keep the responsibility for professionalism with the company, and never pay for substandard service.

WHEN TO CALL SECURITY

Folks often ask me when they should call security, and I always say that whenever you are in doubt of a situation, whether it is overt or just something you suspect, certainly call your officer. If the situation turns out to be nothing or a minor interaction, well, that's good. Security in turn should never chastise a staff member for calling them.

Should you call security every time someone breaks a rule? Of course not. You can embarrass a patron to the point of a verbal confrontation. Do you really need a person with a badge to tell a patron that he can't have a soda by the computer every time you see it happen?

Please remember that having security staff does not mean you can stick your head back in the sand and forget about your own day-to-day security responsibilities. Your security officers cannot be everywhere all the time, no matter how much they walk around. Officers depend on staff to let them know about suspicious behavior as well as overt acts. Nothing got on my nerves more than when, after a behavior problem, an employee commented to me that the person had been acting questionably for a while. Why didn't that staff member give me a heads-up? I was only a phone call away. I never understood that.

Library staff needs to understand and remember that security personnel are there to augment their own awareness and security efforts, not to take the place of them. Staff cannot afford to stop paying attention to their environment just because they have security in the building.

Now ask yourself . . .

Is you security staff visible and vigilant?

Have you set clear expectations?

Do you hold them accountable?

9

PUTTING IT ALL TOGETHER

The one sure way to fail is to try to please everyone.

—Bill Cosby

How SERIOUS ARE you about your security? How serious is your administration? Both are questions only you can answer. I sincerely wish I had some magic answers that would take all your concerns away, but the bottom line is that all of this takes a concerted effort that begins at the top of your organization.

Over the years I was with the library in Charlotte, I had great support from my director. I did not get everything I wanted security-wise, nor did we always agree. On rare occasions (actually, I can only remember two) I was overruled on my decisions with a security incident. When that happened, I simply chalked it up to my boss having an agenda that I was not privy to at my level of management or to him seeing his decision as best for the library. I didn't let it get in the way of the problems of the current day.

Someone told me recently that his director was complaining to him that he was banning too many people. If you have procedures in place and rules for library use, how can you ban too many? If you have the unfortunate luck to have to eject, let's say, three people this week, do you stop and give everyone else a free pass just because you fear reprisal of some type? That is exactly the type of inconsistency that gets you in a world of trouble.

If a patron's behavior gets him ejected, the onus is on him and not the library. Why do libraries see themselves as the troublemakers when someone does not abide by the simple rules of library use? If the next ten people who are ejected are bank vice presidents, for example, then that's just the way it happened. The same goes if they are street people or teachers or wealthy or whatever. *You take them as they come and treat everybody the same.*

Some folks in the library world go to great lengths trying to explain why they don't want to ban patrons permanently, but it is simply the height of irresponsibility to allow some people back into the building. You can talk about the problem patron's rights all day, but what about the rights of other patrons? Don't they have the right to a safe library?

Keep in mind the six things a "black belt" librarian or staff member never does:

1. They never let what they cannot do get in the way of everything they can do.
2. They know that they can control their environment. They learn to feel in charge. They do not let behavior problems dictate the pace of the library.
3. They are problem solvers and are resolved enough to make decisions. They are the "go-to" staff. They never waste time playing the easy role of the critic. Being a constant critic of everything takes no talent. It is so much easier to be critical than correct.
4. They consistently work to simplify and clarify procedures. They do not get caught up in the endless "what if" game.
5. They work to develop and maintain a quiet awareness of their surroundings. They never say that safety and security are someone else's job. Security is everyone's business, period, and they never forget that.
6. They focus on being a real-world team so they can be consistent and have each other's backs.

Stop thinking of security as a separate issue and understand that it is just a vital part of working in any facility that is open to the public in this day and age. It is just part of the process, like good customer service.

These are the common problems I see consistently in my travels.

lack of guidelines for the enforcement of the rules

lack of consistency in enforcement

lack of stringent ban lengths

lack of administrative support

lack of requiring patrons to use the library appropriately

MANAGEMENT

Another vital part of making a library safe is having adequate, effective management. I was far from being the perfect manager, but over the years I have seen quite enough to know that management is a skill that not everyone can learn.

The library world is no different than what I often saw in my previous career in retail management. Some people were good salespeople, and dependable, and maybe they even had business degrees. They were hard workers and everyone liked them. Before you knew it, most of these folks would end up as managers or assistant managers (some were even forced into these positions), and that is where the problems began. They were great employees, but they knew nothing of managing a facility, let alone people.

You have to have the *right managers in the right library branches* before you can even think of how to control the environment. Managers cannot be in denial about what needs to be done to have a safe library. If a manager thinks, for instance, that the answer to patron problems is to say yes to everyone, then you are on the *Titanic,* my friend, and the ice is dead ahead. If you are always going to let patrons have their way and set the pace of your library, why bother to have rules and policies in the first place? The patron is not always right.

A tough branch needs a tough manager, and that is the bottom line. Someone with no leadership or management skills, just a love of books alone, is not going to be able to step up and do what needs to be done with any kind of consistency. I have seen this firsthand over the years. Change to a more effective branch manager and see the various behavior problems miraculously become more controllable.

You also have to have the right managers and frontline staff in those problematic departments. Why work in a branch that has a lot of teens coming in after school if you are afraid of them or have some bias against them?

Another problem I sometimes see in my travels is libraries that have so much internal strife going on that it is impossible for their managers to agree on anything, much less security procedures. This is where the strong manager has to step in and tell them what the ultimate decisions concerning procedures are going to be.

HANDLING AND EVALUATING STAFF

I was asked by a good friend in a library recently if I thought *management* and *leadership* are the same thing. After we shared a laugh over this question being a somewhat typical one in the library world, I answered that yes, of course they were. The best managers I have ever known truly managed staff and led by example.

Part of leadership is letting your staff know what is expected of them and then making sure they are following your lead. So when you have the right training in place and have covered security rules, practices, and good sense all with your staff, what do you do if some of them just won't do their part? I get this question so often that I collated an entire three-hour training session that I now present on management and leadership.

I could never understand staff who were given responsibilities and would not follow through. That just does not compute with me, and not only with regard to security procedures. Some staff fall short in most aspects of their work. Others spend more energy avoiding tasks than it would take to actually complete them.

I was asked once in a seminar by a frontline staff member what to do if one did not agree with policy, did not think it was the correct way of doing things, and did not want to follow the established procedures. My answer to that is simply that you should follow the stated chain of command to voice your complaints, making sure you do not skip any supervisory levels. If at the end of the process things do not change to your liking, you can leave and find another job or you can stay and adjust your perspective and do what is required. Of course, you could also stay and become one of those staff who just complain, condemn, and criticize the management. Do that and you could and should be reprimanded.

Your staff needs to know that not locking your car doors when driving is one thing, not meeting your broader responsibilities on the job is another. By not following the library's security procedures, you endanger not only yourself but everyone else in the building.

You will experience some resistance to some of your procedures. Staff will go along with changes as long as they are not inconvenienced, and some of your procedures will be inconveniences at first. These are sacrifices you and your staff must be willing to make.

You can't control who comes in the door, so why wouldn't all your staff want to work within the library to control things internally as much as possible? If everyone simply tries, you will be pleasantly surprised at what all you can accomplish. This is not a complicated matter, just simple, common sense. Every goal is easier if everyone just does their job.

I can teach any employee, but they have to care in the first place. If they don't care about doing the job and if they don't want to help you, there is not much you can do. If you are in the position to do so, cut your losses and move on with documentation, discipline, and separation if needed.

I have heard some staff say that they "don't want to be police officers," and I can relate, because I didn't want to either. And I wasn't one. Having people skills, maintaining awareness, and being willing to engage are part of working with the public. No matter how you go about a security program, sooner or later everyone is going to have to get up and go over and tell a patron no. That's just the way it is, and everyone should be required to do their part.

One of my strengths as a manager was my simple platform for grading staff. I always measured them by how they performed in three areas: the physical, the ethical, and the attitudinal, or PEA, as I call it.

The physical part of staff members' jobs is simply the way they handle their assigned day-to-day duties. How efficient are they with their work?

The ethical part concerns what they do when you, as their supervisor, are not around. Are they trustworthy or are they stealing? Does their productivity fall when they know you are not there? Do they sit if you want them to stand? Do they avoid and ignore patrons?

The attitudinal part is the third equal part of the pie. How do they interact with the patrons and the other staff? How do they respond to your daily instruction, guidance, and leadership? Are they team players? Do they help or hinder your goals?

A good staff member fulfils all three. Some staff may be great with productivity and they may keep the quality up when you are not present, but if they are constantly complaining or cannot get along with their coworkers, that can be cause for disciplinary action. Others may have a great attitude and you trust them implicitly, but they do not do the basic physical tasks you assign.

The same follows if staff fulfill their actual duties very well—the physical components of their jobs. Everyone likes them and their attitude is always positive, but they cannot be trusted to do the job when you are not immediately supervising them. On your day off, the standard drops. And it is certainly an issue if you think they are taking money or materials from the library.

I simply kept a spiral notebook with pages for each person who reported to me. I always noted dates and time they did an exceptional job and when I praised them for their efforts. I also noted whenever they failed in the areas of the physical, ethical, or attitudinal aspects of their duties as well as times I had to offer counseling or reprimands. These copious but simple notes were all I ever needed to hold my staff accountable, and I never had any issues or problems if termination was ultimately required.

TAKE A LONG look at this chapter. Are you in charge of your facility, or are the patrons? Examining these areas and improving your overall philosophy toward them will bring your security procedures into the real world and give your staff true direction.

Now ask yourself . . .

Is the current way you review staff really accurate?

Do you feel you are in charge of your library?

How serious are you about security and safety in your library?

IN CLOSING

QUESTIONS FOR ALL ON PLANET LIBRARY

I LEAVE YOU with questions of my own that I often asked my friends in the library world. How would you answer them?

Why do we *really* say that libraries are no longer quiet places? How often is that statement based on greatly increased numbers of patrons, computers, or programs—how often on library staff apprehensions about correcting behavior? Is it easier and more convenient to say that the library is "just noisier these days" than it is to approach and tell a patron to lower her voice?

Would we rather say that public behavior is just "getting worse" than make the sustained effort to educate the public about what is simply not allowed in the library? Are you going to give up, or are you and your coworkers going to commit to control your library's environment?

Why is the issue of patron behavior such a hot topic today? Is it because the library's passive approaches just aren't working? Isn't it time to hold the patrons responsible for their behavior? You are a professional and deserve to be treated in a civil manner by the public. Is that really too much to ask? Shouldn't the responsibility for patrons' behavior rest with *them*?

Why do all complaints about patron behavior that result in action have to come from other patrons? Don't the opinions of staff mean anything at all? Can't staff observe and report?

When you say that you "don't want to be a police officer," is that just another way of avoiding telling a patron no?

Are you going to have a plan for security situations, or are you just going to open and hope nothing happens tomorrow morning? Are you just continuing the gambling approach of rolling the dice and seeing what comes up? That is a terrible game you are playing with your safety.

Whatever your existing policy is, does it help or hinder you? Are you in control of the library environment, or are the patrons?

How serious are you about your security? Are you really committed to controlling your library's environment? Does your administration know what it wants, and is it leading the implementation of the plan?

Do you take needless abuse from patrons under the guise of good customer service?

Are you hiding behind a concept of being welcoming? Are you using that as an excuse not to control the library environment?

Here is the thing to remember: *any library environment can be controlled,* and that includes yours. Robert Cannon and I proved that in Charlotte. It can be done and is done in many libraries I have visited.

Of course, I am not saying that my way is the only way, but it is indeed a real-world, proven way. From the concept of library security to an actual functioning plan that works is a huge gap. It is my sincere wish that I help you close that gap.

I LEAVE YOU with one last story:

As you can tell from the content of the book, I gleaned a great deal of guidance from my martial art days. One instructor sat me down after class one evening and drew a circle on a piece of paper. In the middle of the circle, he marked a large dot. "The circle is a hurricane," he explained, "and the dot is the eye of the storm, where everything is calm and serene. In your life, Warren, you need to fight your way through the calamity of the harsh winds to get to the eye and stay there as best you can. As I see you, I think you are always in the storm." He was right. My sixteen-year-old mind could only process this in a literal way, and I had a long way to go before I could actually understand and do what he suggested, but I never forgot it.

Switch now to years later, when Hurricane Hugo came slugging up through South and North Carolina. In Charlotte, I sat through a very long night in my living room as 98 mph winds pounded the front of my house. At one point, the storm stopped and I went outside to take a look. I found out later this was at a point when the hurricane's eye was in my area. Everything was completely still and silent. So help me, I immediately thought about what my old instructor was trying to tell me so many years ago.

We all work through the storms of our life attempting to find a little happiness and contentment. Our jobs, in working with both the public and coworkers, can be the source of great trials and challenges in our life. I finally understood and found the "eye," and I worked hard to get there. I often struggle within myself to stay there. Today, as you unlock the library front door, remind yourself not to let circumstances at work push you back into the chaos of the storm. Keep yourself in the eye. Are you ready?

INDEX